MW00657652

DECONSTRUCTING LUCIFER

DECONSTRUCTING LUCIFER

REEXAMINING *the* ANCIENT ORIGINS *of the* FALLEN ANGEL *of* LIGHT

DAVID W. LOWE

SEISMOS
PUBLISHING
www.earthquakeresurrection.com

Deconstructing Lucifer: Reexamining the Ancient Origins of the Fallen Angel of Light
By David W. Lowe

ISBN-10: 0-61553-386-8
ISBN-13: 978-0-61553-386-5

Published by Seismos Publishing. For more information, visit:
www.earthquakeresurrection.com
www.deconstructinglucifer.com

Printed in the United States of America

October 2011

I Cor 13:2 And if I have prophecy, and *know all mysteries and all knowledge*, and if I have all faith so that I can remove mountains, *but do not have love*...

I am nothing.

CONTENTS

de·con·struct – to examine a piece of writing in order to show that it can be understood in a different way.

INTRODUCTION

WHY WRITE THIS BOOK?

The questions I am most often asked about the books I have written are, "So, why did you write it?" or "What important information is provided in the book that would compel me to care about it?" Having finished writing this book, I offer the following answers to these questions.

1. The Problem of Evil

I believe that answers to the most difficult questions a Christian can face by unbelievers most often involve Lucifer in the end. You will have to get to the end of the book to find out how and why, but it is a product of the desire to ensure that God bears no responsibility for the existence of evil in the world. Examples of these difficult questions include, "If God is such a good God, then how could he allow evil and suffering in the world?" and "Why didn't God just destroy Satan so he couldn't tempt Adam and Eve, and avoid all the evil and suffering that exists?"

These are extremely important questions, and in my opinion, Christians are providing answers that are at best unsatisfactory and at worst misleading or incorrect. The majority of this book will analyze the scriptural evidence for the existence of the fallen angel, Lucifer. But by the end of the book, the reader will be equipped with successful ways to not only explain the problem of evil in the world, but to also skillfully interject the good news of Jesus Christ into the equation. To demonstrate this, two separate hypothetical conversations between an atheist and a Christian are provided.

2. A Desire to Share the Truth

Over the last several years, I have developed a strong aversion to deception in all forms. This resulted from uncovering the truth on a myriad of topics about which I thought I knew the truth, but was only being deceived by powerful interests who ensure the real truth is kept hidden. Having discovered the truth myself, it became my desire to bring the truth to others.

At the heart of evangelism is the Christian's desire to bring truth to a lost and dying world which has never heard it. Paul expressed such a desire in his epistle to the Roman believers, desiring so strongly for his fellow Israelite brothers and sisters to believe in Jesus Christ that he offered to be cut off from Christ himself if they would become believers as a result.[1]

With respect to unbelievers, I desire to deliver the truth of the gospel of Jesus Christ and his position as King of Kings. With respect to believers, I desire to bring the truth of scriptures to light on topics where tradition and emotion have eroded away the truth, such as the one addressed in this book. Paul warned in his second letter to Timothy that people in the future will not tolerate sound teaching of the truth, choosing instead to believe "myths."[2] We must be diligent to study the scriptures to ensure we do not believe myths that are veiled as sound doctrine.

---

[1] See Romans 9:1-5.
[2] See II Timothy 4:3-4.

3. A Love for the Word of God

A third and final justification for writing this book is simply because I love studying the Word of God and uncovering its wonderful and exciting truths about both doctrine and history. Drawn toward study and memorization of the Word of God from an early age, I was privileged to participate in the Assemblies of God Bible Quiz program for seven years. Study and memorization of nearly two-thirds of the New Testament resulted in a love for the Word of God and a desire to continue to learn more of its truths. This picture is one of my favorites, taken in October, 1982 as I lay in my Pac-Man sleeping bag on the living room carpet, studying The Acts of the Apostles.

* * *

While it is exciting to study the *mysteries* of the Word of God, it must be balanced in the life of a Christian with love and evangelism. The verse at the beginning of this book reminds me how much more important it is to have love than to understand all the mysteries in the universe. Paul stated that even if he understood all mysteries but did not have love for God and others, he was nothing.

I would like to thank the following individuals who helped in ways both big and small in the development of this book: Steve Gregg, for his ministry and teaching from the Word of God; Michael Baber, for his excellent paper on Isaiah 14:12; Brenda Mitchell, for her hard work editing; my sister Shari Simon, for listening to me talk about this on the phone and work out the details with her; the many friends I have developed over the years, who have blessed me and encouraged me to continue writing, such as Peter Goodgame, Tony Burtovoy, Derek and Sharon Gilbert, Tom Horn, J. Michael Bennett, David Adams, David Molina, Christopher Warning, Jodi Greiner, Robert Tanner, and many others; my wife Vivienne, for her love and encouragement; and finally, my Lord and Savior Jesus Christ, for redeeming me with his blood, and the Holy Spirit for his inspiration through the Word. It is my sincere hope that this book will be a blessing to you.

David W. Lowe, October 1, 2011

1

LUCIFER RISING

If you are a believer in Jesus Christ as your Lord and Savior, you have heard "The Greatest Story Ever Told" and share it with others. God sent his unique Son, Jesus Christ, into the world to be a sacrifice for the sins of all humanity. He triumphed over his archenemy Satan, the spiritual deceiver and hater of humanity. Jesus Christ suffered and died on a wooden cross and rose from the dead into an immortal body, and his blood cleanses the sin of those who repent of their rebellion against God and put their trust in Christ's sacrifice. He paid the debt for the sin of humanity by experiencing death and shedding His blood in satisfaction for the punishment due for disobeying God's commands. Ultimately and emphatically, he proved his victory over the power of the grave by rising from the dead. We have been delivered from Satan, the one who had the power of death, set forever free from the fear of death!

This victory over Satan, the ancient serpent, was foretold early in the narrative of biblical history. While cursing the serpent in the

Garden of Eden, which The Revelation of Jesus Christ reveals was Satan, God made this famous declaration:

> The LORD God said to the serpent, "Because you have done this, cursed are you above all the wild beasts and all the living creatures of the field! On your belly you will crawl and dust you will eat all the days of your life. And *I will put hostility* between you and the woman and between your offspring and her offspring; her offspring will attack your head, and you will attack her offspring's heel." (*Gen 3:14-15*)

The offspring of the woman was a reference to a future member of the human race who would attack the head of the serpent. Jesus Christ fulfilled this prophecy of victory over Satan by his death and resurrection.

A Pre-Existing Hostility?

Notice that in cursing the serpent, the Lord God established hostility between Satan and the promised seed. "I will *put* hostility between you and the woman…" Does this mean that there would have been no hostility between Satan and Jesus Christ if it had not been divinely established?

Prior to the fall in the Garden of Eden and subsequent curses placed on the serpent, as well as Eve and Adam, the serpent was described as "more shrewd than any of the wild animals that the Lord God had made" (Genesis 3:1). The serpent then proceeded to put Eve to the test, to see whether she would be faithful to God and obey his one commandment. But wasn't there already a pre-existing hostility between Satan and Jesus Christ, who according to scripture was with the Father in the beginning?

In surveying history leading up to the victory at the cross, it is certainly evident that Satan fulfilled the prophecy that he would attack the heel of the woman's offspring. He continuously attempted to kill members of the ancestral line of the promised seed before his head could be crushed, such as his attempt to destroy King David through Goliath, the giant. Jesus Christ, after surviving the command of Herod to kill all male children two years old and under, ultimately met Satan face to face in the wilderness of Judea. There he faced Satan's temptation and later destroyed the power of the enemy through his blood.

So what about this hostility God established between Satan, his offspring, and the offspring of the woman? Why would it be necessary for God to place hostility between them? Wasn't Satan already hostile toward the plan of God at this point? To answer these questions, it will be useful to first understand whether the story of Lucifer is supported in scripture, as well as the orthodox teaching of the church throughout the centuries regarding Lucifer and his rebellion against God.

The Rebellion of Lucifer

It is generally agreed among biblical scholars that angels were created prior to the creation story of Genesis chapter one. A key passage in establishing this understanding is found in Job chapter 38, in which the Lord posed questions to Job regarding the establishment of the earth:

> "Where were you when I laid the foundation of the earth? Tell me, if you possess understanding! Who set its measurements — if you know — or who stretched a measuring line across it? On what were its bases set, or who laid its cornerstone — when the morning stars sang in chorus, and all the sons of God [Hebrew (Hb.) *bên 'ĕlōhiym*] shouted for joy?" *(Job 38:4-7)*

In the Hebrew poetic style of writing, God declared in this passage that when the earth was being established, the sons of God, or *bên 'ĕlōhiym* in Hebrew, were in existence, shouting for joy. Earlier in Job, the *bên 'ĕlōhiym* were present at the throne of God (Job 1:6; 2:1), so it is clear that they are some type of supernatural, angelic beings.

It is widely believed that all of the angels were originally created by God to worship him in heaven, and that they could either remain faithful to God or rebel. In other words, the angels of God were not pre-programmed robots; rather, they were created with a free will just like human beings. According to tradition, one of these angels was named Lucifer. But Lucifer was not your average, run-of-the-mill angel. No, Lucifer was one of three archangels, the other two being Michael and Gabriel. As archangels, they had authority over the other lower-ranking angels. It is believed that each of these three archangels had one-third of the lower-ranking angels following their orders in the heavenly realm.

As the story goes, Lucifer was blessed with unmatched beauty and wisdom among the population of the angels in heaven. He was an anointed guardian angel whose position was to guard the throne of God and protect his holiness. Many believe that Lucifer was also the leader of song and worship before the throne of God. When he sang, he was able to make the most beautiful sounds with the combination of his voice and musical instruments.

But one day, something went very wrong with Lucifer. When God created man in his own image, Lucifer became jealous of man. And when Michael, by divine direction, commanded all the angels to bow down and worship the man God had created, Lucifer was having none of that. Extreme envy and jealousy arose in Lucifer's heart toward man, and he disobeyed God's command to worship Adam.

Because of his unsurpassed beauty and wisdom, the sin of pride arose in Lucifer's heart and he became corrupted. His pride eventually grew to the point that he wanted to overthrow his

Creator God. Lucifer surmised that he could create his own throne and his own kingdom, greater and more powerful than God's. Somehow, he was able to convince one third of the angels in heaven that this overthrow was a possibility.

When God learned of this rebellion, he threw Lucifer and his angels out of the heavenly realm for all eternity. It is believed that at this point Lucifer became Satan the fallen angel, and the angels that followed him became demons. Ever since this pre-historic rebellion, Satan and his demons have been the enemies of God, pure evil, with a fierce hatred for his creation. Although still an angel, tradition teaches that Satan has morphed into a red devil with horns, a tail, and a pitchfork, whose kingdom is in the fiery pits of hell.

Lucifer's Modern Influence

So where did the story of the fall of Lucifer come from? Directly from the divinely-inspired scriptures, we should hope. The teaching is so prevalent among modern day believers that it is considered common knowledge. From the most elite Bible scholars to the laity, the story of Lucifer's fall has become an almost unquestionable theology.

For example, while writing this book, I received a newsletter from a ministry called Elijah's Mantle, an outreach for Christian men affiliated with Perry Stone's Voice of Evangelism in Cleveland, TN. The newsletter content dealt with the original creation and the fall of Lucifer. Below is a short excerpt from the newsletter:

> We also know that God created the heavenly host during this time, including His most cherished angel - Lucifer. Lucifer was perfect in every way. He was the worship leader of the heavenly host. He had everything going for him. In today's vernacular, he would be the guy who was tall, good looking,

> muscular, captain of the football team, class president, and a vice president of a major corporation. So...what happened? He fell! It's easier than you think Brothers! Even though Lucifer had everything going for him...it was not good enough. How do we know this? Isaiah 14 chronicles the Fall of Lucifer. Verse 12 states "How you have fallen from heaven, O star of the morning, son of the dawn!" Why would anyone with such a position and so much going for himself do this? Well, the reason is not so farfetched. Isaiah 14:13 and 14 states that Lucifer said in his heart, "I will ascend to heaven; I will raise my throne above the stars of God, and will sit in the mount of assembly...I will ascend above the heights of the clouds; I will make myself like the Most High." Being everything that he was still was not good enough for Lucifer.[1]

This is a good example of how deeply rooted this theology has become. The author of this newsletter did not consider the content to be controversial or even up for discussion. Isaiah chapter 14 is, you know, that chapter that talks about the fall of Lucifer…everybody knows that, right?

Another example of the modern-day application of the story of Lucifer is the audio series by Dr. Chuck Missler on Genesis titled *Bible Study of Genesis*. Dr. Missler has been a major influence in my life through his many interesting and challenging Bible studies. In this particular audio teaching, he focused on the opening verses of Genesis chapter one:

> The cherubim…were they created? When? See, the question is when were they created. We all accept

---

[1] Excerpt used by permission from Bob Gesing, Elijah's Mantle Ministries, July 2011.

> they were created, but they're not mentioned in Genesis chapter one, unless they're included in verse one, and who knows. Now what makes this even more provocative is we know the one that was in charge, blew it. And we're going to get into that tonight a little bit, and we'll take this occasion to do a little summary review, or what have you, of the origin of one "Lucifer, the anointed cherub that covereth." The guy that was appointed to run things, he was in charge of everything, he led worship. Can you imagine that? He's still trying...the question is, he apparently blew it and fell, right? One third of the angels with him according to Revelation 12. When? See, the problem is, when we see him in Genesis in the garden, he's already fallen.[2]

In introducing a teaching on "The Gap Theory" of Genesis chapter one, Dr. Missler referred to Lucifer as the covering cherubim, and as the leader of worship in heaven. The idea is not considered to be controversial at all, but rather is simply accepted at face value as a foundational theology among believers. Many more examples of the application and acceptance of this teaching by other teachers could be provided. The point is that when the most celebrated and admired Bible teachers of the time teach the story of the fall of Lucifer, those who are being taught simply accept it as fact and repeat it to others.

The story of Lucifer is also a prominent feature of Mormon doctrine. According to the Mormon "Plan of Salvation," all of God's moral creatures are spiritual sons and daughters, including Jesus Christ and Lucifer. It teaches that all people and angels lived as spirits in a pre-mortal existence. As such, we are all brothers and sisters of both Jesus and Lucifer, and Jesus and Lucifer are brothers.

---

[2] Missler, Dr. Chuck, "Genesis 1:2-5," *Bible Study of Genesis* audio download.

Mormon doctrine was illuminated by their "prophet" Joseph Smith, who wrote as follows in one of its holy books, *Doctrines and Covenants*:

> And this we saw also, and bear record, that an angel of God who was in authority in the presence of God, who rebelled against the Only Begotten Son whom the Father loved and who was in the bosom of the Father, was thrust down from the presence of God and the Son, And was called Perdition, for the heavens wept over him—he was Lucifer, a son of the morning. And we beheld, and lo, he is fallen! is fallen, even a son of the morning![3]

According to their theology, Jesus was chosen to bring about God's plan of salvation, and all spirit beings in the heavenly pre-mortal existence were required to give their consent to the plan. When Lucifer's alternative plan was not accepted, he rebelled and convinced one-third of the spirits of heaven to rebel with him.[4]

Religious groups are not the only ones to believe in the existence of Lucifer. Secular groups such as New Age and Masonic authorities not only acknowledge his existence, but have made him the centerpiece of their movements. For example, in September 1887, Luciferian and New Age trailblazer Helena Petrovna Blavatsky first published a journal called *Lucifer*, co-edited by Annie Besant. After 20 volumes and 10 years of publishing, the journal was renamed *The Theosophical Review*.[5] Blavatsky's view was that Lucifer was beneficial to humanity:

---

[3] *Doctrines and Covenants* 76:25-27.

[4] The information regarding Mormon theology was gleaned from "MormonWiki" at http://www.mormonwiki.com/Satan, accessed September 25, 2011.

[5] "Lucifer (magazine)," Wikipedia, the free online encyclopedia, http://en.wikipedia.org/wiki/Lucifer_magazine, accessed August 27, 2011.

> For it is he who was the "Harbinger of Light," bright, radiant Lucifer, who opened the eyes of automaton *created* by Jehovah, as alleged; and he who was first to whisper, "In the day ye eat thereof, ye shall be as Elohim, knowing good and evil," can only be regarded in the light of a Savior. An "adversary" to Jehovah the "*personating spirit*," he still remains in esoteric truth the ever-loving "Messenger"...who conferred on us spiritual, instead of physical immortality–the latter a kind of static immortality that would have transformed man into an undying "Wandering Jew."[6]

The blasphemous Blavatsky regarded Lucifer as a savior, rather than Jesus Christ, whom she regarded as only able to transform man into an "undying wandering Jew." The Theosophical movement built an entire worldview around Lucifer, the light-bringing angel. How could his story, therefore, be anything but true?

Authorities of the Free Masonic movement also incorporated Lucifer into their literature. Albert Pike was an extremely influential leader of Freemasonry, responsible for developing its rituals and writing *Morals and Dogma of the Ancient and Accepted Scottish Rite of Freemasonry* in 1871. In this work, Pike also referred to Lucifer as the "light-bearer:"[7]

> The Apocalypse is, to those who receive the nineteenth Degree, the Apotheosis of that Sublime Faith which aspires to God alone, and despises all the pomps and works of Lucifer. LUCIFER, the

---

[6] Blavatsky, H. P., and B.D. Zirkoff, *The Secret Doctrine*, volume III, p. 243. Theosophical Publishing House, 1993.

[7] "Albert Pike," Wikipedia, the free online encyclopedia, http://en.wikipedia.org/wiki/Albert_Pike, accessed August 27, 2011.

> Light-bearer! Strange and mysterious name to give to the Spirit of Darkness! Lucifer, the Son of the Morning! Is it he who bears the Light, and with its splendors intolerable, blinds feeble, sensual, or selfish souls? Doubt it not! for traditions are full of Divine Revelations and Inspirations: and Inspiration is not of one Age nor of one Creed.[8]

In a section in which Pike explained the Apocalypse, or the Book of Revelation, to freemasonic initiates, he described Lucifer as the "Spirit of Darkness," acknowledging his role as an evil entity, the one who blinds selfish people with his light. Also interesting is the fact that Pike regarded the reference to Lucifer as a "tradition."

As a result of these movements during the nineteenth century, the popularity of 'all things Lucifer' exploded during the twentieth century and into the present century. New Age and Satanic adherents refer to the fallen angel and perform rituals in his honor. Comic books are created based on his legend and his character is portrayed in video games. Songs are written about him and feature films and television shows use his name, such as Kenneth Anger's 1969 film *Lucifer Rising*, which featured Bobby Beausoliel, one of the disciples of Charles Manson ultimately convicted of a murder in 1970.[9]

Lucifer certainly has risen in the consciousness of recent generations, both in believers being aware of his story and unbelievers being deceived by his evil schemes. But despite the popular heights to which this Lucifer has ascended, could it be that his story is just a myth? It is now time to deconstruct Lucifer to determine whether the scriptures support the tradition.

---

[8] Pike, Albert, *Morals and Dogma of the Ancient and Accepted Scottish Rite of Freemasonry*, p. 132. L.H. Jenkins, 1871.

[9] See Wikipedia's "Lucifer in popular culture" for a sampling of how pervasive Lucifer has become in modern times, http://en.wikipedia.org/wiki/Lucifer_in_popular_culture, accessed August 27, 2011.

2

THE LABYRINTH TO LUCIFER

As a child growing up in a Pentecostal, evangelical church, I was taught many "foundations of the faith," most of which I hold fast to this day. In addition, I was taught what are considered non-core interpretations of scripture which at the time I had no reason to doubt. In fact, I had no idea that there was any other way to interpret certain passages, especially passages involving prophecies of the future.

One of the passages of scripture about which I had a firm understanding was Isaiah 14:12-15 based on the King James Version (KJV) of the Bible, the translation with which I grew up. *This is that Old Testament passage about Satan before he fell*, I thought, every time I read it or heard it read to me:

> How art thou fallen from heaven, O Lucifer, son of the morning! how art thou cut down to the ground, which didst weaken the nations! For thou hast said in thine heart, I will ascend into heaven, I will exalt

> my throne above the stars of God: I will sit also upon the mount of the congregation, in the sides of the north: I will ascend above the heights of the clouds; I will be like the most High. Yet thou shalt be brought down to hell, to the sides of the pit. (*Isa 14:12-15 KJV*)

I could tell you nothing about the verses surrounding that passage, nor did I know much at all about Isaiah as a prophetic book of the Bible. But I knew for sure that Lucifer was Satan before he fell and was brought down to hell, and that before he fell, he made the famous five "I will" statements. As far as I knew, there was no other possible interpretation of that passage. I would venture to guess that I am not alone in that position. If a poll were taken of Christians, or even non-Christians, regarding the identity of Lucifer, I would venture a guess that 90% of them would answer "Satan" to that question.

Just reading those verses in a vacuum, it is easy to see how this could be a valid interpretation of the passage. For one thing, the KJV structures the passage to portray that an entity with the proper name of Lucifer was being addressed by the prophet. And everyone knows who Lucifer is, right? In addition, there is no way a human being could make the "I will" boasts. Only a supernatural being with access to heaven could make those boasts. Finally, Lucifer was brought down to hell from the heavens, and Jesus revealed in Luke chapter ten that he saw Satan fall from heaven. It is a pretty airtight argument, an open and shut case, based on the KJV's translation of the passage.

Not only is this interpretation seemingly valid based on the English KJV, but the early church fathers using the Greek and Latin translations, as we will discover, agreed with this interpretation. Thus we have interpreters of three different languages – English, Latin, and Greek – confirming the 'Lucifer is Satan' belief. But what about the original language in which the passage was written: Hebrew?

Investigating the Hebrew "הֵילֵל"

To discern whether this "Lucifer is Satan" interpretation is correct, a thorough understanding of the original Hebrew rendering of Isaiah 14:12 is necessary. "Deconstructing Lucifer" will be a process of subjecting the text to critical analysis in order to determine whether it can be understood in a different way than what has been traditionally understood. In the process, the translations which served to guide readers of the text through the maze that I will call "The Labyrinth to Lucifer" will be thoroughly examined.

This labyrinth is the interpretive, translational maze. It will serve to lead us to an understanding of how the original Hebrew rendering of Isaiah 14:12 eventually led to the interpretation that Lucifer is a name for an angel before he fell and became Satan. The maze begins with the original language in which the passage was written, Hebrew, and continues with the main languages into which it has been translated, which include Greek, Latin, and English. Please see the flowchart near the end of this chapter for a graphic depiction of the progression of the teaching through the various translations.

Below, Isaiah 14:12 is presented in the Hebrew Masoretic text with the word traditionally translated as "Lucifer" in brackets. Keep in mind that Hebrew text is read from right to left:

אֵיךְ נָפַלְתָּ מִשָּׁמַיִם, [הֵילֵל] בֶּן-שָׁחַר; נִגְדַּעְתָּ לָאָרֶץ, חוֹלֵשׁ עַל-גּוֹיִם.

The English transliteration of the verse in Hebrew is presented below, with the word that is traditionally translated as "Lucifer" left untranslated:

Eik nafalta mishamayim הֵילֵל *ben-shachar nigda'ta la'aretz cholesh al-goyim*

The English translation of the verse is presented below, with the word that is traditionally translated as "Lucifer" left untranslated:

> How art thou fallen from heaven, הֵילֵל, son of the morning! how art thou cut down to the ground, which didst weaken the nations! (*KJV*)

The Hebrew word that we must investigate, then, is הֵילֵל. As will be subsequently examined, there is very little Jewish commentary on Satan in the Old Testament. There is even less on whether the passage in Isaiah chapter 14 was an esoteric reference to Satan, and that is because the Jews had no reason to believe there was a reference to Satan to be found. The Jewish understanding of Isaiah chapter 14 was that it was a poetic taunt of the king of Babylon, a prophecy of his imminent downfall.

Continuing the investigation of הֵילֵל, the next stop is the ancient Greek translation. In the third century B.C., King Ptolemy of Egypt commissioned Jewish scholars proficient in both ancient Hebrew and Greek to translate the books of Moses into Greek. Over the next two centuries, the entire Old Testament would be translated into Greek. In modern times, this translation has become known as "The Septuagint," which means 70, the number of Jewish scholars involved in the translation project, and is abbreviated as "LXX."

How did these Jewish scholars translate הֵילֵל into Greek? Isaiah 14:12 is presented below in Greek, from the Masoretic text, as rendered in the LXX. The Hebrew word הֵילֵל traditionally translated as "Lucifer" is underlined:

> πῶς ἐξέπεσεν ἐκ τοῦ οὐρανοῦ ὁ <u>ἑωσφόρος</u> ὁ πρωὶ ἀνατέλλων; συνετρίβη εἰς τὴν γῆν ὁ ἀποστέλλων πρὸς πάντα τὰ ἔθνη.

The English transliteration of the verse in Greek is presented below, with the word that is traditionally translated as "Lucifer" underlined:

> *pos exepesen ek tou ouranou ho* <u>*heosphoros*</u> *ho proi anatello sunetribe eis ten gen ho apostellon pros panta ta ethne*

The English translation of the verse is presented below, leaving the word that is traditionally translated as "Lucifer" untranslated:

> Look how you have fallen from the sky, O *heosphoros*, son of the dawn! You have been cut down to the ground, O conqueror of the nations!

This is an extremely important transition in the meaning of this verse. The LXX translators chose to translate the Hebrew word הֵילֵל as *heosphoros*, which expresses their understanding that the Hebrew word הֵילֵל had the meaning of a shining stellar body.

The English transliteration of הֵילֵל is *heilel.* One possible translation of this word into English would be "shining one." However, the Hebrew root word for *heilel* is a subject of controversy and impacts the proper translation of the word into English. If Isaiah meant to convey a proud and boastful individual, then the root of *heilel* is likely *hālal*, for which the most common translation in the KJV is "to be praised," and "to boast." However, another meaning of *hālal* is "to shine," and evidently it is this meaning that the LXX translators chose in translating הֵילֵל as *heosphoros*. With *hālal* as the Hebrew root, the phrase could be translated into English in either of these fashions:

> Look how you have fallen from the sky! Boast [*heilel*], son of the dawn!

> Look how you have fallen from the sky, o shining one [*heilel*], son of the dawn!

To Shine or To Howl?

However, the controversy is elevated with the understanding that הֵילֵל most likely has a different root word than *hâlal*. This is because הֵילֵל is found in exactly two other verses in the Hebrew Old Testament, and in both instances, הֵילֵל was translated as "howl" from the root verb ילל, transliterated as *yâlal*:"

> Cry and howl [*yâlal;* וְהֵילֵל], son of man: for it shall be upon my people, it shall be upon all the princes of Israel: terrors by reason of the sword shall be upon my people: smite therefore upon thy thigh. (*Eze 21:12 KJV*)[1]

> Howl [*yâlal;* הֵילֵל], fir tree, because the cedar has fallen; the majestic trees have been destroyed. Howl [*yâlal;* הֵילֵל], oaks of Bashan, because the impenetrable forest has fallen. (*Zec 11:2*)

Compare Ezekiel 21:12 and Zechariah 11:2 to Isaiah 14:12, and note that the exact same Hebrew word is found:

> Look how you have fallen from the sky, הֵילֵל [Howl / O shining one], son of the dawn! You have been cut down to the ground, O conqueror of the nations!

Based on the fact that the three other instances in the Hebrew Old Testament in which הֵילֵל appears feature a "howl" translation, the argument could be made that the occurrence in Isaiah 14:12 should also be translated as "howl" if it fits the context of the

---

[1] The word והילל in Ezekiel 21:12 is the same as הילל. It simply has the conjunction v ו [*vav*] prefixed to the beginning of the word. This is equivalent to the English word "and," and the conjunction *vav* is never by itself.

passage. If הֵילֵל should be translated as "shining one," it would be inconsistent with the other three instances in the Hebrew Old Testament in which הֵילֵל is found, where it was translated as "howl" from the root word ילל, or *yâlal*. As for the context of the passage, a "howl" translation fits perfectly, because the king of Babylon was being rebuked by the Lord for his pride, and would be falling from his high estate.

At least two other ancient sources agreed that the passage in Isaiah 14:12 should be translated as "Howl, son of the dawn," instead of "shining one, son of the dawn." Those sources are the Greek translation by Aquila of Sinope and the Syriac Peshitta, a dialect of the Aramaic language. Aquila's Greek rendering of the passage in question is transliterated, then translated into English, as follows, with the word in question underlined in each case:

> *Pos epeses ex ouranou <u>ololuzon</u> huios orthrou*
>
> How have you fallen from heaven! <u>Howl</u> [*ololuzon*], son of the dawn

The Syriac translation is presented below,[2] followed by the English translation, with the word in question underlined in each case:

> ܐܝܟܢܐ ܢܦܠܬ ܡܢ ܫܡܝܐ. [howl] <u>ܐܝܠܠ</u> ܒܨܦܪܐ. ܢܦܠܬ
> ܒܐܪܥܐ ܡܨܚܢ ܠܗ ܕܥܡܡܐ.
>
> How have you fallen from heaven! <u>Howl</u> [ܐܝܠܠ] in the morning, you who fell to the ground, reviler of the nations!

---

[2] Baber, Michael. *Discourse: The Latin Word Lucifer*, http://parshanuth.blogspot.com, accessed May 21, 2011. Both the Aramaic Peshitta and English rendition of Isaiah 14:12 were used by permission of the author.

The Syriac text of Isaiah 14:12 contains the verb ܐܝܠܠ (*'ilal*) which is from the root verb ܝܠܠ (*yilal*), and means "to howl." This translation was confirmed by Adam Clarke in his Commentary on the Bible:

> The Versions in general agree in this translation, and render הֵילֵל *heilel* as signifying Lucifer, *Φωσφωρος*, the morning star, whether Jupiter or Venus; as these are both bringers of the morning light, or morning stars, annually in their turn…I doubt much whether our translation be correct. הֵילֵל *heilel*, which we translate Lucifer, comes from יָלַל y*ālal*, yell, howl, or shriek, and should be translated, "Howl, son of the morning;" and so the Syriac has understood it…[3]

In addition, the preeminent translator of the ancient Hebrew scriptures into the Latin language, St. Jerome, confidently declared that the proper translation of *heilel* was "howl:"

> For greater ease of understanding we translated this passage as follows: "How you have fallen from heaven, Lucifer, who arose in the morning." But if we were to render a literal translation from the Hebrew, it would read, "How you have fallen from heaven, howling son of the dawn."[4]

Even so, St. Jerome made the decision "for greater ease of understanding" to translate the word as *lucifer* in Latin, probably because the Greek LXX translators understood the word to be not the adjective "howl," but rather the noun *heosphoros*, or the bright shining planet Venus.

---

[3] Clarke, Adam. Commentary on the Bible, Isaiah 14:12.
[4] Jerome, Commentary on Isaiah 5.14.12–14, cited and translated in Steven A. McKinion, editor, Ancient Christian Commentary on Scripture: Old Testament, volume 10, p. 121. Downers Grove, IL: InterVarsity Press, 2004.

If a "howl" translation had been used, then "The Labyrinth to Lucifer" would never have been traversed. Why? Because that labyrinth begins with translating the original Hebrew הֵילֵל into Greek as *heosphoros* instead of *ololuzon*, a Greek verb meaning "howl." As has been shown, the only three other occurrences of הֵילֵל in the Hebrew Masoretic Text of the Old Testament were translated with the Greek verb which means "howl," not an adjective such as "shining." This is a strong argument against a *heosphoros* translation.

What is *Heosphoros*?

Notwithstanding this evidence, the *heosphoros* translation of the LXX prevailed. We must therefore proceed down the labyrinth from that point to discern how our understanding of Lucifer developed using that word. That translation, again, is rendered as follows:

> Look how you have fallen from the sky, *ho heosphoros*, son of the dawn! You have been cut down to the ground, O conqueror of the nations!

What, then, is the meaning of *heosphoros*? About this there is no mystery and no controversy. *Heosphoros* was used many times in both the LXX Old Testament as well as the Greek New Testament. It means "bringer of the dawn," but its common translation into English is "morning star" and was always used as an epithet for the planet Venus. *Heosphoros* is found seven times in the LXX translation (including Isaiah 14:12), and is translated into English each time as "morning star" or "morning." Consider the following examples:

> Let the stars of that night be darkened; let it remain dark, and not come into light; and let it not see the

> morning star [*heosphoros*] arise: (*Job 3:9, Brenton LXX*)
>
> Or did I order the morning light in thy time; and did the morning star [*heosphoros*] then first see his appointed place; (*Job 38:12, Brenton LXX*)
>
> At his sneezing a light shines, and his eyes are as the appearance of the morning star [*heosphoros*]. (*Job 41:18, Brenton LXX*)

In each of these passages, *heosphoros* was translated as "morning star." We can gain an understanding about the usage of this word from secular ancient Greek writers, who often referred to either *heosphoros* or *eosphoros*, a variant spelling, or to *hesperos*. In each case, they were referring to the evening star, the planet Venus, which reaches its maximum brightness shortly before the sunrise and shortly after the sunset.[5]

A bit of confusion enters the equation with the understanding that the Greeks seemingly used interchangeable words for the planet Venus because they understood the evening and morning appearances of the planet to be two different stars. In Greek mythology, Hesperos was known as the evening star, the planet Venus in the evening. Hesperos was the son of Eos and the brother of Eosphoros, also known as Phosphoros. Phosphoros is another name for the planet Venus, as it appears in the morning, i.e. the morning star.[6]

Hesperos, as the planet Venus in the evening, and Eosphoros/Phosphoros, as the planet Venus in the morning, are sometimes seen as one since they are personification of the same

---

[5] "Hesperus, Redirected from Heosphoros," Wikipedia, The Free Encyclopedia, http://en.wikipedia.org/wiki/Hesperus, accessed May 8, 2011.
[6] *Ibid.*

physical planet, Venus. In Greek, *eosphoros* means "bringer of the dawn," and *phosphorus* means "bearer of light."[7]

One ancient Greek writer who provides some clarity on the usage of *heosphoros* was Philo Judaeus, who wrote as follows in *The Decalogue*:

> . . . for they call the earth Proserpine, and Ceres, and Pluto. And the sea they call Neptune, inventing besides a number of marine deities as subservient to him, and vast companies of attendants, both male and female. The air they call Juno; fire, Vulcan; and the sun, Apollo; the moon, Diana; and the evening star [*heosphoron*], Venus [*Aphroditen*] . . .[8]

According to Philo in this passage, *heosphoros* was known to the ancient Greeks as the planet Venus. The English translator of this passage chose to translate *Aphroditen*, a reference to the Greek goddess Aphrodite, as "Venus" since Venus is the Roman equivalent to the Greek Aphrodite, but a proper translation into English would have been "Aphrodite," not Venus. Regardless of the translation, it is clear that the planet Venus was meant by Philo.

Another ancient Greek writer was Marcus Tullius Cicero, who wrote about the planets in *De Natura Deorum* (*On the Nature of the Gods*) as follows:

> The lowest of the five wandering stars, and the one nearest the earth, is the planet of Venus, which is called Φωσφόρος [*Phosphoros*] in Greek, and Lucifer in Latin, when it is preceding the sun, but Ἕσπερος [*Hesperos*] when it is following it; it completes its course in a year, traversing the zodiac

[7] *Ibid.*

[8] Philo Judaeus, *The Decalogue*, Section 54, as translated into English by Charles D. Yonge.

> both latitudinally and longitudinally, as is also done by the planets above it, and on whichever side of the sun it is, it never departs more than two signs' distance from it.[9]

According to Cicero in this passage, the planet Venus was known by two different Greek names: Phosphoros when it is preceding the sun and Hesperos when it is following the sun. A few additional ancient Greek scholars provide all the more proof that Venus, the morning star, is the meaning of *heosphoros*, including Homer, Plato, and Hesiod:

> But at the hour when the star of morning [*heosphoros*] goeth forth to herald light over the face of the earth—the star after which followeth saffron-robed Dawn and spreadeth over the sea—even then grew the burning faint, and the flame thereof died down. And the winds went back again to return to their home over the Thracian sea, and it roared with surging flood.[10]

> . . . Thus far, at least, I asseverate with certainty: I say, once more, that there are eight of them, and that while three of the eight have been told, five yet remain. The fourth in motion and transit together, and the fifth, are almost equal to the sun in speed, and on the whole are neither slower nor swifter. These being three, must be so regarded by him who has sufficient mind. So let us speak of them as powers of the sun and of Lucifer [*heosphorou*], and

[9] Marcus Tullius Cicero, *De Natura Deorum*, Book 2, Section 20.53, as translated by Francis Brooks; London: Meuthen, 1896.

[10] Homer. *The Iliad* with an English Translation by A.T. Murray, Ph.D. in two volumes. Cambridge, MA., Harvard University Press; London, William Heinemann, Ltd., 1924.

> of a third, such that we cannot express it in a name because it is not known . . .[11]

> And Eos bore to Astraeus the strong-hearted winds, brightening Zephyrus, and Boreas, headlong in his course, and Notus,—a goddess mating in love with a god. And after these Erigeneia bare the star Eosphorus [*heosphoron*], and the gleaming stars with which heaven is crowned.[12]

The three preceding quotations all associate the Greek word *heosphoros* with the planet Venus in some fashion, whether as the "star of morning" by Homer, "Lucifer" or "Venus" by Plato, or "the star Eosphoros" by Hesiod. Note that the translator of Plato's *Greater Hippias* used a transliteration of "Lucifer" instead of a proper translation of "Venus," because the Latin word *lucifer* had become so common that it was interchangeable with the planet Venus.

With this brief, if not somewhat confusing, journey through the Greek translation of *heosphoros* now complete, "The Labyrinth to Lucifer" edges closer to the end with the Latin Vulgate translation, yet another important predecessor to the English language.

Lucifer: Satan or Venus?

The Latin word *lucifer* is a compound of *lux*, meaning "light," and *fero*, meaning "to bear." Prior to being transliterated as "Lucifer" in the early English translations of Isaiah 14:12, the word had no meaning in the English language. In Latin, however, the word was used commonly for the planet Venus, also known as the "morning

---

[11] Plato. *Epinomis, 986e*. Plato in Twelve Volumes, Vol. 9 translated by W.R.M. Lamb. Cambridge, MA, Harvard University Press; London, William Heinemann Ltd. 1925.

[12] Hesiod. *Theogony, 375-380*, The Homeric Hymns and Homerica with an English Translation by Hugh G. Evelyn-White. Theogony. Cambridge, MA.,Harvard University Press; London, William Heinemann Ltd. 1914

star" or "day star." In the Latin Vulgate translation of both the Old and New Testaments, the word *lucifer* was used numerous times.

First, let us examine the only three Old Testament verses in which the Latin word *lucifer* is used to translate the Greek word *heosphoros*, and compare them to the English translation of the LXX:

> And thy prayer shall be as the morning star [Lt. (Latin) *lucifer*; Gr. (Greek) *heosphoros*], and life shall arise to thee as from the noonday. (*Job 11:17, Brenton LXX*)
>
> With thee is dominion in the day of thy power, in the splendours of thy saints: I have begotten thee from the womb before the morning [Lt. *luciferum*; Gr. *heosphorou*]. (*Psa 110:3 Brenton LXX*)
>
> How has Lucifer [Lt. *lucifer*; Gr. *heosphoros*], that rose in the morning, fallen from heaven! He that sent orders to all the nations is crushed to the earth. (*Isa 14:12, Brenton LXX*)
>
> How art thou fallen from heaven, O Lucifer [Lt. *lucifer*; Gr. *heosphoros*], son of the morning! how art thou cut down to the ground, which didst weaken the nations! (*Isa 14:12, KJV*)

Notice the inconsistency in the translation. Even though the Latin Vulgate and Greek LXX use *lucifer* and *heosphoros* to translate all three verses, the English translation uses different terms: "morning star" or "morning," and "Lucifer." The following chart illustrates the inconsistency of both the English translation of the Septuagint and the KJV:

Passage	Greek (LXX)	Latin Vulgate	English (LXX)
Job 11:17	*heosphoros*	*lucifer*	"morning star"
Psalm 110:3	*heosphorou*	*luciferum*	"morning"
Isaiah 14:12	*heosphoros*	*lucifer*	"Lucifer"

A clear example of how inappropriate it is to translate the Latin *lucifer* into a nonexistent English word "Lucifer" is found in Peter's second epistle:

> Moreover, we possess the prophetic word as an altogether reliable thing. You do well if you pay attention to this as you would to a light shining in a murky place, until the day dawns and the morning star [(Lt.) *lucifer*; (Gr.) *phosphoros*] rises in your hearts. (*II Pet 1:19*)

Notice that the English translation of the Latin *lucifer* and Greek *phosphoros* in this passage was "morning star," and in this case, Peter was clearly referring to Jesus Christ as the morning star ("day star" in the KJV), comparing him to the planet Venus as it rises in the morning. Recall that the Greeks referred to the planet Venus as *phosphoros* when it precedes the sun in the morning, and in this verse, Peter made some interesting comparisons and allusions to the coming of Jesus Christ involving the planet Venus.

First, he compared the prophetic word to a light, and the world in which we live to a dark place. Second, he referred to the dawning of the day and the appearance of the morning or day star, an allusion to the coming of Jesus Christ at the dawning of the day just as *phosphoros*, or Venus, makes it appearance in the morning. The word *phosphoros* is a compound of *phos*, meaning "light," and *phero*, meaning "to bring" or "to bear." In other words, Peter called Jesus Christ the light-bringer, comparing him to Venus in the morning. In Revelation 22:16, Jesus confirmed this to be a valid designation by declaring himself to be the bright shining star of the morning.

Now, how inappropriate would it be to translate the Latin *lucifer* in this verse as “Lucifer” instead of “morning star” or “daystar?” Consider how this verse would read with that translation:

> Moreover, we possess the prophetic word as an altogether reliable thing. You do well if you pay attention to this as you would to a light shining in a murky place, until the day dawns and Lucifer rises in your hearts. (*II Pet 1:19*)

This translation from Latin into English would give Jesus Christ the inappropriate and confusing title of “Lucifer.” And yet, this is exactly what the translation of Isaiah 14:12 accomplishes with the title of “Lucifer” given to the king of Babylon. Both titles are wholly erroneous based on the analysis presented in this chapter.

In addition to the biblical proof that the Latin word *lucifer* is a reference to the planet Venus, there are countless usages of the word by ancient Latin writers. A few clear examples include selected quotations from the writings of Pliny and Seneca:

> Below the sun revolves a very large star named Venus [*veneris*], which varies its course alternately, and whose alternative names in themselves indicate its rivalry with the sun and moon—when in advance and rising before dawn it receives the name of Lucifer [*luciferi*], as being another sun and bringing the dawn, whereas when it shines after sunset it is named Vesper [*vesper*], as prolonging the daylight, or as being a deputy for the moon. This property of Venus was first discovered by Pythagoras of Samos

about the 42nd Olympiad, [612-609 BC] 142 years after the foundation of Rome. Further it surpasses all the other stars in magnitude, and is so brilliant that alone among stars it casts a shadow by its rays.[13]

The colours of the planets vary with their altitudes, inasmuch as they are assimilated to the stars into whose atmosphere they come in rising, and the circuit of another's path modifies their colour in either direction as they approach, a colder circuit to pallor, a hotter one to redness, a windy one to a leaden colour, the sun and the intersection of its orbit with theirs, and also the extremities of their paths, changing them to black darkness. It is true that each has its own special hue—Saturn white, Jupiter transparent, Mars fiery, Lucifer [*Lucifero*] bright white, Vesper glaring, Mercury radiant, the moon soft, the sun when rising glowing and afterwards radiant; with these being causally connected also the appearance of the fixed stars.[14]

Like as the daystar [*lucifer*] from on high scatters the stars of night, As, when the stars return again, clear Hesper brings his light, Or as the ruddy dawn drives out the dark, and brings the day, As the bright sun looks on the world, and speeds along its way His rising car from morning's gates: so Caesar doth arise, So Nero shows his face to Rome before the people's eyes, His bright and shining countenance

---

[13] Pliny. *Natural History*, Book II, Chapter 6, §36, as translated by H. Rackman, W. H. S. Jones, and D. E. Eichholz. Harvard University Press, MA and William Heinemann, London: 1949-54.
[14] *Ibid*, Chapter 16, §79.

> illumines all the air, While down upon his graceful neck fall rippling waves of hair." Thus Apollo.[15]

Just as it was in the previously-cited scriptures, *lucifer* was used by these ancient Latin authors to describe the planet Venus, translated as "the daystar," or transliterated as "Lucifer" in English by modern translators. There can scarce be any doubt, then, that the meaning of the Latin word *lucifer* was used in every case for the planet Venus when it precedes the sun in the morning sky, and never for any physical or spiritual person, at least not until the final stop on "The Labyrinth to Lucifer" was reached: the early English translations of the Bible.

Early English Translations[16]

The first English translation of the Bible was handwritten from the Latin language by John Wycliffe in 1395. Wycliffe's astounding effort was written in an early form of English called Middle English, and his source was the Latin Vulgate translation. The Wycliffe Middle English rendition of Isaiah 14:12 is presented below, followed by a modern English rendition of each word:

> A! Lucifer, that risidist eerli, hou feldist thou doun fro heuene; thou that woundist folkis, feldist doun togidere in to erthe.
>
> Ah! Lucifer, that rises early, how you have fallen down from heaven; you that wounded folk has fallen down together into earth.

[15] Seneca. *Apocolocyntosis*, §3.379, as translated by W. H. D. Rouse, 1920.
[16] All of the history of the early English versions of the Bible as presented in this section was based upon the timeline found at GreatSite.com, and excellent source for a history of the printed Bible. Accessed from http://www.greatsite.com/timeline-english-bible-history/index.html, September 2, 2011.

Here begins the morphing of the Latin word *lucifer* into an English word "Lucifer" with this maiden English translation. As was explained above, a direct and proper translation of *lucifer* into English is "light-bearer." However, because the common use of *lucifer* in Latin was a reference to the planet Venus when it precedes the sun in the sky, an acceptable English translation would be "morning star" or "daystar." But Wycliffe chose to *transliterate*, not *translate*, the Latin *lucifer* into English with the creation of an English word "Lucifer."

What could have motivated Wycliffe's transliteration? Perhaps the English word for the planet Venus had not yet been developed, and so, knowing that *lucifer* was a clear Latin reference to Venus, he chose to transliterate the Latin word as "Lucifer" in English. It is not clear why Wycliffe chose this transliteration, but according to *The Barnhart Dictionary of Etymology*, the English word "Lucifer" was "borrowed from Latin *lucifer* the morning star."[17] Thus, "Lucifer" in English originated wholly from the Latin, and means "morning star," which is an epithet for the planet Venus. There is no indication that Wycliffe meant anything other than a reference to the planet Venus with this transliteration. Wycliffe provided a clue in another passage in which he translated the Latin word *luciferum* as "Lucifer" in English:

> Whether thou bryngist forth Lucifer [Lt. *luciferum*; Hb. *mazzârāh*; Gr. *maxsuroth*], 'that is, dai sterre, in his tyme, and makist euene sterre to rise on the sones of erthe?' (*Job 38:32, Wycliffe*)

In this verse, the author of Job used the Hebrew word *mazzârāh* which has generally been understood as a reference to the constellations in one form or another. The Latin translation simply used *luciferum*, a reference to the planet Venus, which was

[17] Barnhart, Robert K. *The Barnhart Dictionary of Etymology*, p. 619. The H. W. Wilson Company, 1988.

followed by Wycliffe in his English translation. Regardless of whether the planet Venus or the constellations as a whole were indicated by the writer of Job, it is clear from the context of the passage that some kind of stellar or planetary reference was meant. Thus, a title for Satan of "Lucifer" in Isaiah 14:12 in Wycliffe's translation, rather than a stellar or planetary reference, is wholly unwarranted.

The distinction of the first printed complete Bible in the English language goes to the Coverdale Bible, published in 1535 by Myles Coverdale and John Rogers. For the Old Testament Hebrew scriptures, the authors used the German Bible published by Martin Luther, as well as the Latin Vulgate. The Latin version of Isaiah 14:12 has been covered in depth, but what about the German translation of Martin Luther?

> *WJe bistu vom Himmel gefallen du schöner Morgenstern* [you beautiful morning star]*? Wie bistu zur Erden gefellet der du die Heiden schwechtest?*[18]

The German translation, as did the previous translations, properly translated the phrase as a reference to the "morning star," or the planet Venus. Thus, these authors had two translations as their sources, each of which clearly made a reference to the planet Venus with the Latin *lucifer* and the German *Morgenstern.* But notice that Luther capitalized this word for morning star, giving it a proper name designation. Could this, along with the Wycliffe early translation into Middle English and the interpretations of the Ante-Nicene Church Fathers (to be explored in the chapters to follow), have been enough influence on Coverdale and Rogers to translate the first English version of the Old Testament as they did? The Coverdale Bible rendition of Isaiah 14:12 is presented below:

[18] The German Bible of Martin Luther provided by Lutherbibel.net at http://lutherbibel.net, accessed May 17, 2011. Translation into English by Yahoo! Babel Fish at babelfish.yahoo.com, accessed May 17, 2011.

> How art thou fallen from heauen (O Lucifer) thou faire mornige childe? Hast thou gotten a fall even to the grounde, thou that (notwithstandinge) dyddest subdue the people?

Additional early English translations include (a) The Matthew's Bible (1537) by John Rogers, which was the first English translation of the Old and New Testaments based on the original Hebrew, Aramaic, and Greek texts; (b) The Great Bible (1539) by Myles Coverdale, the first English Bible authorized for public use; (c) The Geneva Bible (1560) led by John Calvin and John Knox, the first Bible to incorporate verse numbers; (d) Bishop's Bible (1568) produced by the Church of England from the original Hebrew, Aramaic, and Greek texts; (e) The Douay/Rheims Bible (1609), produced by the Roman Catholic Church solely from the Latin Vulgate language; and finally, (f) The King James Version (1611), commissioned by King James, led by Desiderius Erasmus, among other contributors, and based upon the original Hebrew, Aramaic, and Greek languages.

Each of these translations (a) – (f) are presented below, with the marginal notes as presented in the original text, if available:

> (a) <u>The Matthew's Bible</u> (1537) How art thou fallen from heaue (O Lucifer*) thou fayre mornynge chylde? hast thou gotten a fell eue to the grounde thou (notwithstandyng) dydest subdue the people?
> * He compareth the death of Nabuchedonoso to the fallyng of Lucifer the mornynge sterre, which he calleth the chylde of the mornynge…

> (b) <u>The Great Bible</u> (1539) Howe art thou fallen from heauen, (O Lucifer) thou fayre mornynge chylde? howe haste gotten a fall euen to the grounde, arte become weaker then the people?

(c) The Geneva Bible (1560) How art thou fallen from heauen, O Lucifer*, sonne of the morning? and cutte downe to the grounde, which didest cast lottes vpon the nations?
* You who thought yourself most glorious and as it were placed in the heaven for the morning star that goes before the sun, is called Lucifer, to whom Nebuchadnezzar is compared.

(d) Bishop's Bible (1568) Howe art thou fallen from heauen O Lucifer, thou faire mornyng chylde? Howe hast thou gotten a fall euen to the grounde, which didst weaken the nations?

(e) The Douay/Rheims Bible (1609) How art thou fallen from heaven, O Lucifer*, who didst rise in the morning? how art thou fallen to the earth, that didst wound the nations?
* O Lucifer. . .O day star. All this, according to the letter, is spoken of the king of Babylon. It may also be applied, in a spiritual sense, to Lucifer the prince of devils, who was created a right angel, but fell by pride and rebellion against God.

(f) King James Version (1611) How art thou fallen from heauen, O Lucifer, sonne of the morning? how art thou cut downe to the ground, which didst weaken the nations?
* Or, a daystarre.

Note that in each case where the translation provides a marginal note, with the exception of the Roman Catholic Douay/Rheims translation, the reference to "Lucifer" was explained as the morning star or daystar, that goes before the sun – a clear reference to the planet Venus, and consistent with the Greek and Latin translations. These key marginal notes from four very early English translations provide clear and convincing evidence concerning what the word "Lucifer" meant to English speakers in the sixteenth and early seventeenth centuries. Among these early English translations, though, only the Roman Catholic Douay/Rheims Bible makes the connection of "Lucifer" to Satan, making it clear that Lucifer, in their view, is the proper name of "the prince of devils" before his rebellion.

The Douay/Rheims English translation was an "if you can't beat 'em, join 'em" response by the Roman Catholic Church to the early Protestant English translations. Prior to this, the Roman Catholic Church attempted to keep the Bible in the Latin language and out of the hands of the common people, reasoning that they should not interpret the scriptures for themselves. Seeing that the English versions were gaining in popularity, the Roman Catholic Church decided that if an English language Bible were to be produced widespread, they wanted the influence of the Roman Catholic Church upon it. *Using only the Latin Vulgate language as a source*, not the original languages, the Douay/Rheims English translation was produced. The footnote to Isaiah 14:12 as shown above served to perpetuate for the Roman Catholic Church the "Satan is Lucifer" interpretation.

The following chart presents "The Labyrinth to Lucifer" as traversed in this chapter. Note that there are two directions to be taken from the beginning of the chart: the one to the left which leads to a "Lucifer" translation, and the one to the right which leads to a "howl" translation, of the Hebrew word הֵילֵל, or *heilel*. The dominant translation through the centuries has been to the left side, leading to "Lucifer," but it is not necessarily correct. As was previously shown, the Hebrew word הֵילֵל is found three times in the Hebrew Old Testament: Isaiah 14:12, Ezekiel 21:12, and Zechariah 11:2 (twice). In each case, the word is translated as the verb "howl," except for Isaiah 14:12, where the inconsistent translation of "morning star," "daystar," and "shining one" were selected and have ruled the day.

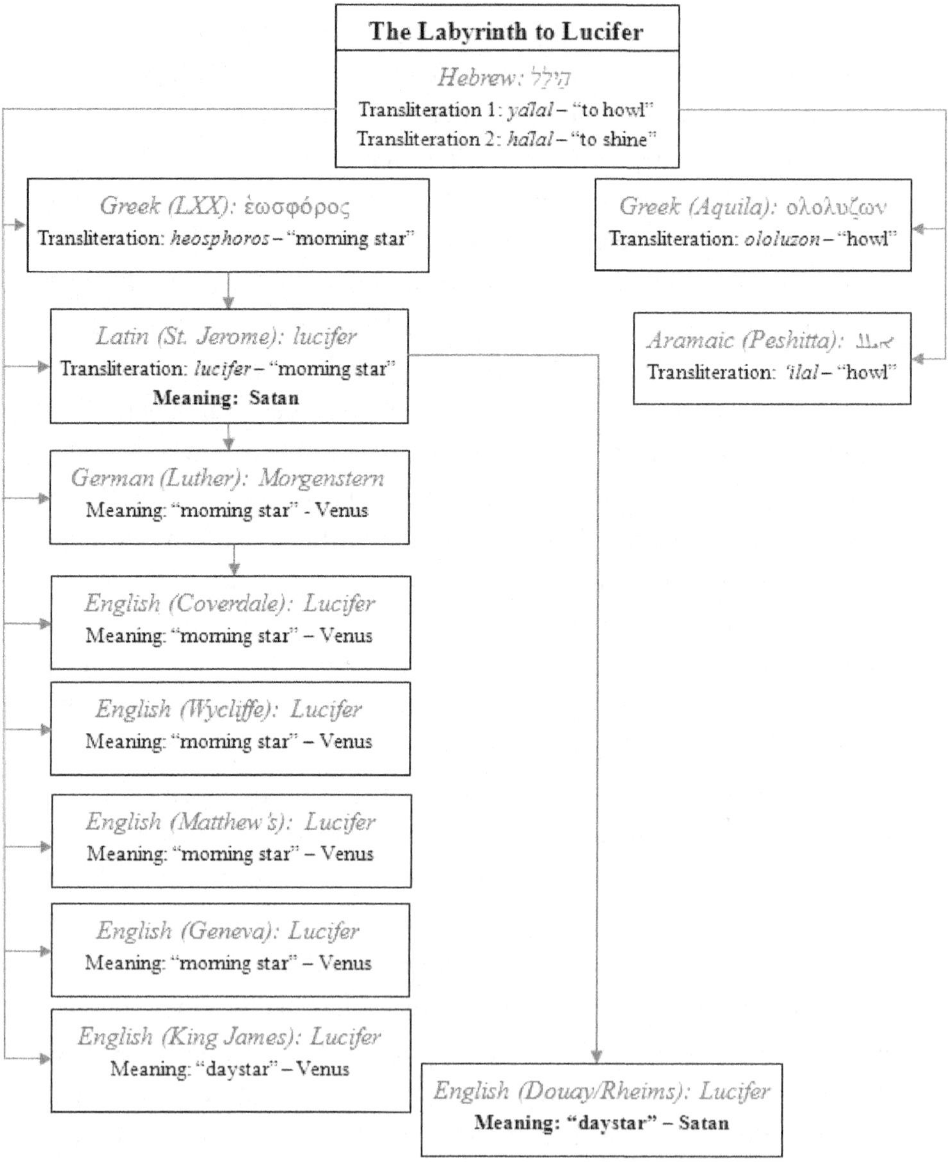

Summary

The key points to be taken from this important chapter are:

- The translation of the Hebrew *heilel* into the various languages is the subject of controversy, because it is unknown from which root word it is derived. The two possibilities are *hâlal*, which can mean "to shine," and *yâlal*, which means "to howl."
- The Hebrew הֵילֵל is found in exactly two other verses in the Old Testament, and in both instances was translated into English in the verb form, "to howl." Only the Isaiah 14:12 features הֵילֵל with a noun, "to shine."
- The Hebrew הֵילֵל, transliterated into English as *heilel*, was translated in the LXX as *heosphoros*, which is a reference to a shining stellar body. The LXX translators, therefore, decided that the root of *heilel* was *hâlal*, "to shine." This was a key turning point in the meaning of this verse to future generations.
- At least two other sources chose to follow the other Old Testament passages in which *heilel* was translated with the verb *yâlal*, "to howl." Those sources were the translation of Aquila of Sinope and the Syriac Peshitta, a translation using the Aramaic language. St. Jerome also declared that "howl" was the correct translation, but still chose *lucifer* in his Latin translation.
- The Greek *heosphoros* means "morning star," and is a clear reference to the planet Venus as it appears in the morning sky before the dawn.
- There are three Old Testament passages in which the Greek *heosphoros* was translated into Latin as *lucifer*, or "morning star:" Job 11:17, Psalm 110:3, and Isaiah 14:12. In the English translations of these verses, only Isaiah 14:12 renders the word as "Lucifer" in English, while the other two verses render the word as "morning star."

- The word "Lucifer" as it is appears in English translations had no meaning, but was simply a transliteration from the Latin language for the word *lucifer*, which also means "morning star" and is a reference to the planet Venus.
- Martin Luther's German translation from the Latin language rendered Isaiah 14:12's *lucifer* as *Morgenstern*, or "morning star."
- Early English translations from the Hebrew, Greek, and Latin translations rendered Isaiah 14:12's as "Lucifer," but provided the explanation that the word meant "morning star" or "day star," a reference to the planet Venus.
- Only the Roman Catholic Douay/Rheims translation into English provided the margin explanation that "Lucifer" was a veiled reference to Satan, the prince of the devils.

This translational journey labeled "The Labyrinth to Lucifer" is very important in order to understand how the current understanding of Isaiah 14:12 evolved. It is very likely, in my understanding of the evidence, that the correct translation of הֵילֵל is actually "howl," not "Lucifer." However, the "shine" translation won the day given the influence of the LXX. It is now time to begin an interesting search for the first person to understand Isaiah 14:12 as a reference to Satan.

3

THE "LUCIFER PRIMER"

In the 1997 motion picture *Contact*, a mysterious message intercepted by SETI (Search for Extraterrestrial Intelligence) scientists was thought to have been sent from intelligent beings from another world. One of the scientists, Dr. Eleanor Arroway, played by actress Jodie Foster, searched for a hidden code within the message, which contained both audio and visual data. When the key that unlocked the hidden code was revealed to her by another retired scientist, she exclaimed, "You found the primer!" Based on the primer (pronounced "primmer"), they could understand the message and construct a machine that, it was thought, would take them to the beings from whom the message originated.

Similarly, there is a key that I believe will help in the quest to understand the source of the story of Lucifer. The goal is to discover the first mention of the entity, what I call "The Lucifer Primer," from early Jewish or Christian witnesses. This primer will allow us to understand how the teaching began and provide clarity surrounding its progression through the centuries.

There are many scriptures that are used to substantiate the story of Lucifer, both in the Old and New Testaments. We will get to those scriptures shortly, carefully dissecting them to get to the truth. But who was the first to teach this belief? Was it taught by pre-Christian Jewish rabbis or scholars? Or was it an interpretation put forth first by the early church fathers in a post-New Testament timeframe? Which early church fathers believed this teaching, and how has it survived with such strong support to the present day?

Evidently, there were several stages of development in arriving at the story of the rebellion of Lucifer. Beginning with the earliest Jewish sources, continuing through the early church fathers, and concluding with Origen, the tradition was increasingly expanded upon until a full-featured story was fleshed out in works such as Milton's *Paradise Lost* and Dante's *Inferno*. Perhaps more enlightening than the early church fathers that developed the story of the fall of Lucifer, which will be examined in detail, are those earlier witnesses who made no mention of Lucifer, a fall of Satan, or the idea that he was once a fallen angel.

Early Jewish Sources

Beginning with the understanding of Jewish authorities on the biblical text, Lucifer was definitely not a name ascribed to Satan, simply because the word "Lucifer" had no meaning in the Hebrew language. The entity known as Satan was simply a spiritual being who was an adversary or hinderer to God's people. According to the Jewish Encyclopedia, Satan's actions in the Old Testament characterize him as a "member of the divine council who watches over human activity, but with the evil purpose of searching out men's sins and appearing as their accuser."[1] Examples of this behavior include the only three times Satan is named in the Old Testament: the testing of Job (Job chapters one and two), the testing

---

[1] Jacobs, Joseph and Ludwig Blau. "Satan," Jewish Encyclopedia.com. http://www.jewishencyclopedia.com/view.jsp?artid=270&letter=S#ixzz1JjNVbjtH, accessed April 16, 2011.

of David to number Israel (I Chronicles chapter 21), and the accusing of Joshua the high priest (Zechariah chapter three). However, the Jewish Encyclopedia is void of any connection of Satan with an entity named Lucifer. Under the entry "Lucifer," the story is labeled a "myth" derived from works such as *The Life of Adam and Eve* and *Slavonic Enoch*, which most scholars consider to be post-Christian works and which will be investigated later. In addition, the entry states that the Lucifer myth was perpetuated by early church fathers such as Tertullian and Origen.[2]

Another important Jewish source for a clue regarding their understanding of the existence of a fallen angel named Lucifer is the Septuagint (LXX) Greek Old Testament. As previously discussed, the LXX Greek translation of the Hebrew *heilel ben-shachar* of Isaiah 14:12 is *heosphoros*, which means "bringer of the dawn" and is a reference to the planet Venus, the morning star.[3] Believing that Isaiah was comparing the king of Babylon to a stellar, god-like being in the Hebrew poetic style of writing, the LXX translators reasoned that the origin of *heilel* was the primitive root *hâlal*, one of the meanings of which is "to be clear" or "to shine." In addition, they reasoned that the Hebrew *shachar* was from the primitive root *shâchar*, which means, "to dawn" or "to be early." A translation of *heilel ben-shachar* into Greek, therefore, was rendered *heosphoros*, the morning star, which is an epithet for the planet Venus.

Continuing with a survey of the work of Jewish commentators Philo Judaeus (20 BC-50 AD) and Flavius Josephus (37-100 AD), there is no help to be found. These men, famous for their lengthy expository treatment on the ancient Old Testament scriptures, rarely mentioned Satan since he was not a major figure of the Old

---

[2] Kohler, Kaufmann. "Lucifer," Jewish Encyclopedia.com. http://www.jewishencyclopedia.com/view.jsp?artid=612&letter=L, accessed September 3, 2011.

[3] "Hesperus" Wikipedia, The Free Encyclopedia, http://en.wikipedia.org/wiki/Eosphoros, accessed April 16, 2011.

Testament. As for their commentary on the serpent of Genesis chapter three, they do not connect the serpent with Satan but instead seem more concerned with how an animal could speak. Keep in mind that the Christian association of the serpent with Satan is only found in The Revelation of Jesus Christ, chapters 12 and 20, which these men did not have the opportunity to consider due to its late authorship and inclusion in the New Testament.

The Babylonian Talmud and the Targum are commentaries on the Hebrew Old Testament that were accumulated and recorded from the first century after Christ until the end of the first millennium. These later Jewish sources are very helpful in our quest for "The Lucifer Primer" because they provide commentary on the same Isaiah chapter 14 passage that we examined in the LXX. Specific quotations reveal that the Jews, even well after the time of Christ and the early church fathers, understood that the passage was referring only to the king of Babylon:

> It is written [Isaiah xiv. 12]: "How art thou fallen from heaven, O morning-star, son of the dawn! how art thou hewn down to the ground, crusher of nations!" ("Crusher" is expressed by the word "Cholesh," and the inference is made from the supposition that lots were cast which nation was to be crushed first.) It is written [Daniel iv. 33]: "And additional greatness was added unto me." What was that additional greatness? Said R. Jehudah in the name of R. Jeremiah bar Aba: 'From this we can infer, that he (Nebuchadnezzar) rode a male lion and twisted a snake round the lion's head, to verify what is written [Jeremiah xxvii. 6]: 'And also the beasts of the field have I given him to serve him.''[4]

[4] Babylonian Talmud, *Tractate Pesachim*, Chapter 9.

> But the nations of the world do not act thus. When I bestowed greatness upon Nimrod, he said, Come, let us build us a city [Genesis 11:4]; upon Pharaoh, he said, Who is the Lord? [Exodus 5:2]; upon Sennacherib, he said, Who are they among all the gods of the countries? [2 Kings 18:35]; upon Nebuchadnezzar, he said, I will ascend above the heights of the clouds [Isaiah 14:14][5]

> How art thou cast down from on high, who wast shining among the sons of men as the star Venus among the stars: thou art dashed down to the earth, who wast a slaughterer among the nations.[6]

Each of these sources confirm the Jewish understanding that the entity being addressed was the king of Babylon (whom they believed to be Nebuchadnezzar) and that the prophet Isaiah was, in a taunting poetic form, comparing his lofty status before his fall to the morning star, the planet Venus.

The Fall of the Watcher Angels

A well-known story of angelic rebellion among both the Jews and the early church fathers is recorded in *I Enoch: Book of the Watchers*, as well as several other sources. *I Enoch* is a work whose authorship is disputed, although the book itself claims to have been authored by Enoch, the seventh from Adam. However, most scholars doubt that Enoch authored the work and instead date the work approximately 300 years before the birth of Christ. My belief is that Enoch could have originally recorded the visions in the *Book of the Watchers*, and the work was preserved and expanded upon through the generations.

---

[5] Babylonian Talmud, *Tractate Chullin*, Chapter 6.

[6] *The Chaldee Paraphrase on the Prophet Isaiah (by Jonathan B. Uzziel)*, translated by C. W. H. Paul. London: London Society's House, 1871.

There are several other books in the *Enoch* series, most of which scholars date well after the birth of Christ and some into the seventh century, but the *Book of the Watchers* is viewed as the most authentic and trustworthy of the group. This is due to the fact that, in addition to being the earliest book of *Enoch* in the series, it is directly quoted in the canonized scriptures. Jude's epistle provides the quotation from *I Enoch* chapter one:

> Now Enoch, the seventh in descent beginning with Adam, even prophesied of them, saying, "Look! The Lord is coming with thousands and thousands of his holy ones, to execute judgment on all, and to convict every person of all their thoroughly ungodly deeds that they have committed, and of all the harsh words that ungodly sinners have spoken against him." *(Jud 14-15)*

Compare this with the passage from *I Enoch* chapter one:

> And behold! He cometh with ten thousands of His holy ones to execute judgment upon all, And to destroy all the ungodly: and to convict all flesh of all the works of their ungodliness which they have ungodly committed, and of all the hard things which ungodly sinners have spoken against Him. (*I Enoch 1:9*)

Jude's direct quotation from the *Book of the Watchers* proves that at the very least he was familiar with the text, and that he considered the writing to be authoritative, though it does not necessarily prove he believed it rose to the level of inspired scripture. I believe Jude's quotation establishes the writing as a trustworthy source for historical information, and for expanding upon certain portions of the canonized scripture. However, because its authorship could not be absolutely verified, it should not be included as part of the canonized scripture. It is interesting to point out, though, that *I Enoch: Book of the Watchers* was quoted in the Dead Sea Scrolls found in Qumran,[7] and is considered canon by the Ethiopian Orthodox Church and the Eritrean Orthodox Church, both in northeast Africa.[8]

There are some who believe that there is a connection between a fall of Lucifer along with one-third of the angels, and the angels who sinned, as recorded in Genesis chapter six, II Peter chapter two, Jude, and the *Book of the Watchers*. However, based on the text of the *Book of the Watchers*, this can be completely ruled out.

The story of the sin of the angels begins in the *Book of the Watchers* chapter six, in which a Watcher angel named Semjaza convinced a group of fellow Watcher angels to commit sin with human women, 200 angels in all. They came down from heaven onto Mount Hermon in the days of Jared, whom Genesis chapter five records as the sixth generation from Adam and the father of Enoch. The text states that these angels began to lust over the beauty of human women and decided they wanted to choose women to bear children for them. In addition to defiling themselves sexually with the women, they taught them all types of other esoteric skills which apparently had not yet been revealed to them. These skills included charms, enchantments, herbal medicines, metalworking, weaponry, all types of physical adornment, coloring tinctures, and the use of all types of precious stones. Most of these skills were revealed by one of the 200 Watcher angels named Azazel.

The *Book of the Watchers* refers to the offspring of the human woman and angels as giants due to their extreme size and height.

---

[7] Clontz, T.E. and J., "*The Comprehensive New Testament with complete textual variant mapping and references for the Dead Sea Scrolls, Philo, Josephus, Nag Hammadi Library, Pseudepigrapha, Apocrypha, Plato, Egyptian Book of the Dead, Talmud, Old Testament, Patristic Writings, Dhammapada, Tacitus, Epic of Gilgamesh*", Cornerstone Publications, 2008, p.711.

[8] "Book of Enoch" Wikipedia, The Free Encyclopedia, http://en.wikipedia.org/wiki/I_Enoch, accessed July 13, 2011.

When these hybrid offspring had consumed all of the produce that humanity could sustain, they turned on humanity itself and the animal kingdom and began to consume them, including drinking their blood. The holy angels Michael, Uriel, Raphael, and Gabriel, who did not defile themselves with the fallen Watcher angels, brought all these things before the Lord God of heaven, and he began to pronounce a judgment against the Watchers. Azazel was sentenced to be cast into darkness in the desert of Dudael and covered with rocks until the "day of great judgment," at which point he would be cast into the fire. As for the other 199 angels, their sentence was to be bound for 70 generations in the "valleys of the earth," after which they would join Azazel in the abyss of fire. Stiff sentences indeed.

There are several clues within the *Book of the Watchers* account itself that completely rule out the possibility that the author was attempting to chronicle an ancient rebellion and fall of Lucifer, or that the sin of Semjaza and the other Watcher angels was in any way connected with a fall of Lucifer:

- Only 200 select Watcher angels, not one third of all the angels of heaven, fell into sin.
- These events are stated to have happened in the days of Jared, who according to Genesis chapter five lived well after the creation of Adam. Thus, this could not be referring to a heavenly rebellion during the days of Adam.
- The angel Semjaza led the rebellion in lusting after human women, rather than Lucifer leading a rebellion as a result of jealously and pride.
- Azazel, another Watcher involved in the rebellion, was one of the main instigators, and the Lord said to "ascribe all sin" to Azazel. This same name is found in Leviticus chapter 16, where the Lord instructed Moses to cast the sin of the Israelites on one of two goats, the scapegoat or

Azazel. The *Book of the Watchers* reveals that this angel's punishment was to be thrown into the wilderness abyss of Dudael, and the Lord told Moses to let the scapegoat depart to Azazel in the wilderness. Some believe Azazel to be another name for Satan since the sin of the Israelites was to be placed on him, but Satan was never sentenced to be cast into the wilderness in Dudael. Thus it is clear that Azazel and Lucifer/Satan are not the same entity.

- In *I Enoch* chapter 54, Satan is named separately in the story of the fallen angels. Note that Azazel and the other rebellious angels were subject to Satan, thus indicating that Satan was a separate entity from both Semjaza and Azazel and that this angelic rebellion had nothing to do with any heavenly rebellion of Lucifer:

> These are being prepared for the hosts of Azazel, so that they may take them and cast them into the abyss of complete condemnation, and they shall cover their jaws with rough stones as the Lords of Spirits commanded. And Michael, and Gabriel, and Raphael, and Phanuel shall take hold of them on that great day, and cast them on that day into the burning furnace, that the Lord of Spirits may take vengeance on them for their unrighteousness *in becoming subject to Satan* and leading astray those who dwell on the earth. (*I Enoch 54: 4, 6*)

Based on these clues, it is clear that the story of the sin of the angels as recorded in Genesis chapter six, II Peter chapter two, Jude, and *I Enoch: Book of the Watchers* was a separate fall of Watcher angels. Therefore, a connection between a fall of an entity named Lucifer and one third of the angels and the story in the *Book of the Watchers* can be completely ruled out.

With this brief investigation of the early Jewish sources complete, it can be confidently stated that "The Lucifer Primer" is not to be found in their commentaries or extra-biblical writings. Beginning with *I Enoch: Book of the Watchers*, to the LXX, to the commentaries of Philo Judaeus and Flavius Josephus, to the Talmud and Targum, no reference to Lucifer can be found. The only clue we found was in the Jewish Encyclopedia, which called Lucifer a myth designed by early church fathers.

The Ante-Nicene Fathers

The first Council of Nicaea took place in 325 AD in what is modern-day Turkey, authorized by the Roman Emperor Constantine I. It was an effort to reach a consensus among Christians with respect to all matters of faith and doctrine. The early church fathers which provided commentary on the scriptures prior to this Council are referred to as the Ante-Nicene Fathers, and are considered the earliest Christian witnesses after the actual authors of the New Testament.

Will "The Lucifer Primer" be found in the commentaries and letters of the Ante-Nicene Fathers? One of the earliest of these early church fathers was Ignatius, and prior to his work, very few clues can be found on the topic of Satan and his origins in the works which have survived to this day. A survey of the letters and commentaries of Clement (30-100 AD), Mathetes (130 AD), Barnabas (100 AD), Polycarp (65-155 AD), and Papias (70-155 AD) are void of any reference to Satan as a fallen angel. Beginning with Ignatius, the first clues regarding the development of the story regarding the origins of Satan as a fallen angel are revealed.

<u>Ignatius (30-107 AD)</u>

Ignatius was the first of the early church fathers to make a connection between Satan and fallen angels. In his epistle to the believers of the city of Philippi, he made two references that indicate a belief in Satan's status as an angel who had been cast out of heaven:

> Darest thou, then, who didst fall "as lightning" from the very highest glory, to say to the Lord, "Cast thyself down from hence" to whom the things that are not are reckoned as if they were, and to provoke to a display of vainglory Him that was free from all ostentation?[9]

> Thou, O Belial, dragon, apostate, crooked serpent, rebel against God, outcast from Christ, alien from the Holy Spirit, exile from the rank of angels, reviler of the laws of God, enemy of all that is lawful, who didst rise up against the first-formed of men, and didst drive forth the commandment that who had in no respect injured thee; thou who didst raise up against Abel the murderous Cain; thou who didst take arms against Job: dost thou say to the Lord, "If thou wilt fall down and worship me?"[10]

There are two items of which to take note from these passages. First, Ignatius believed that Satan at one point in history was in the very highest glory, with the Lord in heaven. He used Luke 10:18, in which Jesus stated that he saw Satan fall as lightning from heaven, as a proof text of this belief. Second, Ignatius believed that Satan was a "rebel from heaven" and an "exile from the ranks of the angels." Both of these reference points indicate Ignatius' belief in an early rebellion of Satan from heaven, and that he was once an angel, key data points in the story of the rebellion of Lucifer.

---

[9] Ignatius. *The Epistle of Ignatius to the Philippians*, Chapter 10-Continuation: Audacity of Satan.

[10] *Ibid*, Chapter 11-Continuation: Audacity of Satan.

Justin Martyr (110-165 AD)

Another early church father who provided clues to the prevalent belief about Satan's origins was Justin Martyr, who followed after Ignatius. One of his writings was quoted by Irenaeus, a later church historian and commentator, and reveals one of Justin's beliefs about Satan:

> Truly has Justin remarked: That before the Lord's appearance Satan never dared to blaspheme God, inasmuch as he did not yet know his own sentence, because it was contained in parables and allegories; but that after the Lord's appearance, when he had clearly ascertained from the words of Christ and His apostles that eternal fire has been prepared for him as he apostatized from God of his own free-will, and likewise for all who unrepentant continue in the apostasy, he now blasphemes, by means of such men, the Lord who brings judgment [upon him] as being already condemned, and imputes the guilt of his apostasy to his Maker, not to his own voluntary disposition.[11]

From this statement, the belief of Justin Martyr regarding Satan's rebellion is evident. He believed that Satan "voluntarily departed from God" and fell away of "his own will and predilection." The most compelling and revealing quotation from Justin Martyr, however, is found in his *Hortatory Address to the Greeks*. In chapter 28, titled "Homer's Obligations to the Sacred Writers," he made the argument that the Greek poet Homer used the writings of Moses in Genesis to craft his mythological stories,

---

[11] Irenaeus. *Against Heresies*, Chapter 26-John and Daniel Have Predicted the Dissolution and Desolation of the Roman Empire, Which Shall Precede the End of the World and the Eternal Kingdom of Christ. The Gnostics Are Refuted, Those Tools of Satan, Who Invent Another Father Different from the Creator.

including the story of the creation, the Garden of Eden paradise, and the Tower of Babel. In addition, Justin Martyr believed that a fall of Satan from heaven was referenced by Homer in the classic mythological work *The Iliad*:

> And the same holds good regarding the enemy of mankind who was cast out of heaven, whom the Sacred Scriptures call the Devil, a name which he obtained from his first devilry against man; and if any one would attentively consider the matter, he would find that the poet, though he certainly never mentions the name of "the devil," yet gives him a name from his wickedest action. For the poet, calling him Ate, says that he was hurled from heaven by their god, just as if he had a distinct remembrance of the expressions which Isaiah the prophet had uttered regarding him. He wrote thus in his own poem: —
>
> "And, seizing by her glossy locks
> The goddess Ate, in his wrath he swore
> That never to the starry skies again,
> And the Olympian heights, he would permit
> The universal mischief to return.
> Then, whirling her around, he cast her down
> To earth. She, mingling with all works of men,
> Caused many a pang to Jove." [emphasis added][12]

We found the primer! Although he does not mention the name Lucifer simply because the word had no meaning outside of the Latin language, this commentary marks the first time among all the commentaries I carefully surveyed in this study that the fall of Satan was associated with a prophecy written by Isaiah. Thus, it is

---

[12] Justin Martyr. *Hortatory to the Greeks*, Chapter 28-Homer's Obligations to the Sacred Writers.

this reference that we can call "The Lucifer Primer," the interpretational embryo, so to speak, that eventually grew into the fully developed tradition we know today. The key is his reference to an unidentified passage by the prophet Isaiah, which he declared revealed a truth about the fall of Satan and that "he was hurled down from heaven." Without question, that unidentified passage was Isaiah chapter 14, in which the prophet wrote a taunting message in poetic writing style to the king of Babylon:

> Look how you have fallen from the sky, O shining one, son of the dawn! You have been cut down to the ground, O conqueror of the nations! You said to yourself, "I will climb up to the sky. Above the stars of El I will set up my throne. I will rule on the mountain of assembly on the remote slopes of Zaphon. I will climb up to the tops of the clouds; I will make myself like the Most High!" But you were brought down to Sheol, to the remote slopes of the pit. *(Isa 14:12-15)*

This clue leads me to conclude that it was an established belief at the time of Justin Martyr, who wrote during the second century and was influenced by earlier church fathers, that the Isaiah chapter 14 passage not only registered a scathing rebuke to the king of Babylon, but also was meant to convey historic facts about an ancient fall of Satan from heaven. It is particularly telling that Justin Martyr did not deem it necessary to cite or quote the passage from Isaiah to which he was referring. This further strengthens the argument that it was an already firmly established interpretation that Isaiah was referring to Satan's rebellion in this passage. From a chronological perspective, Justin Martyr's joining of the Satanic rebellion with the passage from Isaiah chapter 14 is the first among the church fathers whose writings were preserved.

Summary

Let us now take an inventory of the clues that we have discovered thus far in the quest to find the origin of the belief that Lucifer was once a beautiful heavenly angel that rebelled against God and was cast from heaven. It has been thus far established that:

- Early Jewish teaching was devoid of the belief that Satan was a fallen angel, but rather focused on his role in the Old Testament of an accusing adversary.
- In the third century before Jesus Christ's birth, the LXX translated the key passage in Isaiah 14:12 from *heilel ben-shachar* in Hebrew to *heosphoros* in Greek, a reference to the morning star, Venus.
- Neither Philo nor Josephus, Jewish historians who wrote just prior to and after Jesus Christ, made mention of Satan as a fallen angel, nor did they connect the devil to Isaiah 14:12.
- Important early church fathers which preceded Ignatius and Justin Martyr, such as Clement, Mathetes, Polycarp, Barnabas, and Papias, made no mention of Satan being a fallen angel.
- Ignatius first used Jesus' statement in Luke 10:18, "I saw Satan fall like lightning from heaven" to connect Satan with a being who was once an obedient angel, but rebelled.
- Justin Martyr was the first early church father to connect Isaiah 14:12 to Satan falling from heaven. This is "The Lucifer Primer," the key clue in the progression to the fully-developed Lucifer tradition, as no recorded commentary among the early church fathers before him made a connection between Isaiah 14:12 and Satan.

Let us continue this exploration of the early understanding regarding the connection of Satan to Isaiah 14:12 as recorded by the Ante-Nicene church fathers. As time progressed away from the doctrine of the apostles, the theology of Lucifer began to evolve and move further into the realm of speculation.

4

The Proliferation Intensifies

With this foundation established, the early church fathers to follow will continue to build on the idea that Satan was once a good heavenly angel who rebelled based on Isaiah chapter 14 and other passages. Among the additional clues to be revealed, it will be discovered that the proper name "Lucifer" was first used more than two centuries after Jesus Christ's birth.

Irenaeus (120-202 AD)

Writing in a later time frame than Ignatius and Justin Martyr, early church father Irenaeus made similar statements, but with an important additional clue. In *Against Heresies*, he wrote at length regarding his understanding of the origins of Satan, including the following passages:

The Lord, indeed, sowed good seed in His own field; and He says, "The field is the world." But while men slept, the enemy came, and "sowed tares in the midst of the wheat, and went his way." Hence we learn that this was the apostate angel and the enemy, because he was envious of God's workmanship, and took in hand to render this [workmanship] an enmity with God. For this cause also God has banished from His presence him who did of his own accord stealthily sow the tares, that is, him who brought about the transgression;[1]

Just as if any one, being an apostate, and seizing in a hostile manner another man's territory, should harass the inhabitants of it, in order that he might claim for himself the glory of a king among those ignorant of his apostasy and robbery; so likewise also the devil, being one among those angels who are placed over the spirit of the air, as the Apostle Paul has declared in his Epistle to the Ephesians, becoming envious of man, was rendered an apostate from the divine law: for envy is a thing foreign to God. And as his apostasy was exposed by man, and man became the [means of] searching out his thoughts (*et examinatio sententioe ejus, homo factus est*), he has set himself to this with greater and greater determination, in opposition to man, envying his life, and wishing to involve him in his own apostate power.[2]

---

[1] Irenaeus. *Against Heresies, Book IV,* Chapter 40-One and the Same God the Father Inflicts Punishment on the Reprobate, and Bestows Rewards on the Elect.
[2] Irenaeus. *Against Heresies, Book V,* Chapter 24- Of the Constant Falsehood of the Devil, and of the Powers and Governments of the World, Which We Ought to Obey, Inasmuch as They Are Appointed of God, Not of the Devil.

Recall that one feature of the Lucifer story was that he was jealous of God's creation, Adam, and for this cause was cast from heaven with one third of the angels. Here, Irenaeus revealed his understanding that Satan was "envious of God's workmanship" and was banished from the presence of God because of this trait. As will be shown later, Irenaeus was probably influenced by *The Life of Adam and Eve*, as this is a near direct quotation from that work. Irenaeus also called Satan an "apostate angel," meaning that Satan was at one time an angel in heaven and in good standing with God, but rebelled.

In the second passage, Irenaeus makes the connection between Satan and Ephesians 2:2. In that verse, Paul revealed there is a spiritual entity that is energizing the children of disobedience, a "spirit of the air," and Irenaeus declared that this spiritual entity is Satan.

Tertullian (145-220 AD)

Accelerating the progression toward what is presently understood about Lucifer, Tertullian was the first of the early church fathers to connect a prophecy in Ezekiel chapter 28 to Satan in his writings. In *Against Marcion*, in which Tertullian argued against a man whom he considered a heretic, he wrote as follows:

> Now, whence originated this malice of lying and deceit towards man, and slandering of God? Most certainly not from God, who made the angel good after the fashion of His good works. Indeed, before he became the devil, he stands forth the wisest of creatures; and wisdom is no evil. If you turn to the prophecy of Ezekiel, you will at once perceive that this angel was both by creation good and by choice

> corrupt. For in the person of the prince of Tyre it is said in reference to the devil…[3]

Note that Tertullian, similar to the early church fathers before him, declared the devil to have been a good angel who became evil. To support this point, Tertullian continued by citing a passage from Ezekiel that was addressed to the prince of Tyre. He was the first among the writings of the early church fathers to shift the traits from the earthly leader of Tyre to Satan:

> Son of man, sing a lament for the king of Tyre, and say to him, 'This is what the sovereign LORD says: 'You were the sealer of perfection, full of wisdom, and perfect in beauty. You were in Eden, the garden of God. Every precious stone was your covering, the ruby, topaz, and emerald, the chrysolite, onyx, and jasper, the sapphire, turquoise, and beryl; your settings and mounts were made of gold. On the day you were created they were prepared. I placed you there with an anointed guardian cherub; you were on the holy mountain of God; you walked about amidst fiery stones. You were blameless in your behavior from the day you were created, until sin was discovered in you. In the abundance of your trade you were filled with violence, and you sinned; so I defiled you and banished you from the mountain of God — the guardian cherub expelled you from the midst of the stones of fire.' (*Eze 28:11-16*)

Tertullian continued, explaining the meaning of these verses as they applied, in his opinion, to Satan:

---

[3] Tertullian. *Against Marcion, Book II,* Chapter 10- Another Cavil Met, i.e., the Devil who Instigated Man to Sin Himself the Creature of God. Nay, the Primeval Cherub Only Was God's Work. The Devilish Nature Superadded by Wilfulness. In Man's Recovery the Devil Is Vanquished in a Conflict.

> This description, it is manifest, properly belongs to the transgression of the angel, and not to the prince's: for none among human beings was either born in the paradise of God, not even Adam himself, who was rather translated thither; nor placed with a cherub upon God's holy mountain, that is to say, in the heights of heaven, from which the Lord testifies that Satan fell; nor detained amongst the stones of fire, and the flashing rays of burning constellations, whence Satan was cast down like lightning. No, it is none else than the very author of sin who was denoted in the person of a sinful man: he was once irreproachable, at the time of his creation, formed for good by God, as by the good Creator of irreproachable creatures, and adorned with every angelic glory, and associated with God, good with the Good; but afterwards of his own accord removed to evil.[4]

By assigning the Ezekiel chapter 28 passage to Satan, Tertullian essentially declared that Satan:

- Was born in the paradise of God, in heaven,
- Fell from heaven after being among the starry constellations,
- Was once a sinless angel before God

With this association, the origins of Satan progressed far beyond any of the previous Jewish commentators or early church fathers. Why did Tertullian feel justified in connecting the passage from Ezekiel chapter 28 with Satan? According to his own words, the poetic prophecy of Ezekiel was so lofty and supernatural that it could not be applied to a mere human being, in this case, the king

[4] *Ibid.*

of Tyre. In doing so, did Tertullian strip Ezekiel of his prerogative to use exaggeration and hyperbole within the Hebrew poetic style of writing in order to make a point about the pride of the earthly leader of Tyre? Or was he justified in his interpretation? These questions will be addressed as we progress.

Origen (185-254 AD)

One of the most prolific writers of the Ante-Nicene period, Origen was a scholar of both the Hebrew and Greek languages. He originally hailed from the church of Alexandria but was excommunicated for heretical teaching. Because of this, many did not regard him as an early church father. Some did, however, including Eusebius, the renowned church historian. Among some of the extreme actions taken by Origen was self-castration based on a literal interpretation of Matthew 19:12, an act confirmed by Eusebius.

Origen was known for interpreting scripture in ultra-allegorical fashion, reasoning that while it had a primary literal meaning, there was also an esoteric secondary meaning that must be carefully mined and considered by the reader. Origen was obsessed with discovering these esoteric meanings, to the point of incredulity in some cases.

The first excerpt from the writing of Origen to consider is perhaps the most important. Writing in the third century after all of the aforementioned authors, Origen made the following declaration in the Preface of *De Principiis (On First Principles)*:

> Regarding the devil and his angels, and the opposing influences, the teaching of the Church has laid down that these beings exist indeed; but what they are, or how they exist, it has not explained with sufficient clearness. This opinion, however, is held by most, that the devil was an angel, and that, having become an apostate, he induced as many of the angels as

> possible to fall away with himself, and these up to the present time are called his angels. [emphasis added][5]

The important consideration in this quotation is that Origen admitted that the following teachings about the devil, or Satan, are only opinions that cannot be firmly supported in scripture:

- The devil was once a holy angel of God
- This holy angel became an apostate
- The apostate angel induced other angels to fall away with him

Though only opinions and not based on scripture, these are the same arguments held by his predecessors. Origen confirmed that the opinions were widely held in the early church.

Among Origen's accomplishments as a Hebrew scholar was a re-translation of the Septuagint, as well as commentaries in the Greek language. The English translation of Origen's Greek commentaries was provided by Rev. Frederick Crombie in 1869. Rev. Crombie translated the following passage from Origen's commentary *De Principiis* using "Lucifer" for the Greek *heosphoros* in assigning a proper name to the devil prior to his fall:

> Again, we are taught as follows by the prophet Isaiah regarding another opposing power. The prophet says, "How is Lucifer [*heosphoros*], who used to arise in the morning, fallen from heaven…" Most evidently by these words is he shown to have fallen from heaven, who formerly was Lucifer [*heosphoros*], and who used to arise in the morning. For if, as some think, he was a nature of darkness, how is Lucifer [*heosphoros*] said to have existed

[5] Origen. *De Principiis, Book I,* Preface, 6.

> before? Or how could he arise in the morning, who had in himself nothing of the light? Nay, even the Saviour Himself teaches us, saying of the devil, "Behold, I see Satan fallen from heaven like lightning." For at one time he was light[6]

This marks the first occurrence in the Ante-Nicene literature in which the Greek *heosphoros*, translated into English as "Lucifer" by Rev. Crombie, is equated with the devil. Origen reasoned that Isaiah 14:12 was meant to be a hidden reference to the ancient fall of Satan by citing Luke 10:18, in which Jesus stated, "I saw Satan fall as lightning from heaven," just as Ignatius before him. Later in the same work, Origen provided more interpretive clues:

> In a similar manner also, what is spoken of the prince of Tyre cannot be understood of any man or king of Tyre. And how could we possibly accept, as spoken of a man, what is related in many passages of Scripture, and especially in Isaiah, regarding Nebuchadnezzar? For he is not a man who is said to have "fallen from heaven," or who was "Lucifer [*heosphoros*]," or who "arose in the morning."[7]

Here Origen declared that both the Ezekiel chapter 28 and Isaiah chapter 14 passages addressing the prince of Tyre and the king of Babylon were veiled references to the fall of Lucifer, or the devil. In his view, the content of these passages simply could not be taken to describe any human being in a literal fashion.

Let us pause again to take an inventory of the clues provided by Irenaeus, Tertullian, and Origen regarding the tradition of Lucifer, the fallen angel, as presented in this chapter:

---

[6] Origen. *De Principiis, Book I,* Chapter V-On Rational Natures, 5.
[7] Origen. *De Principiis, Book IV,* Chapter I, 22.

- Irenaeus taught that the devil was once an angel in heaven, but was banished from God's presence. This shows Irenaeus was likely influenced by an identical story recorded in *The Life of Adam and Eve*.
- Tertullian was the first early church father to assign the passage in Ezekiel chapter 28 to Satan, reasoning that the entity being addressed simply could not be human due to the descriptions by the prophet.
- Origen declared that the church's teachings about the devil (that he was once an angel who later rebelled and induced other angels to fall with him) were only opinions circulating in the church, not facts based on scripture.
- Origen was the first to assign a proper name to an entity in Isaiah 14:12, *heosphoros*, and declare it to be a reference to the devil. Rev. Frederick Crombie translated Origen's work into English, and provided a translation of the Greek *heosphoros* using the word "Lucifer."

Vita Adae et Evae and Slavonic Enoch

The Ante-Nicene church fathers may have been influenced by two pseudepigraphal works in their interpretation of the pertinent passages from Isaiah chapter 14 and Ezekiel chapter 28. The first is *Vita Adae et Evae*, or *The Life of Adam and Eve*, a work about which scholars disagree regarding authorship and date. Most scholars agree that it was probably Jewish in origin, although some believe it could have been written by Christians. As for the date of authorship, some scholars believe it was written between the third and seventh centuries. However, The Jewish Encyclopedia stated, "The Lucifer myth was transferred to Satan in the pre-Christian century, as may be learned from *Vita Adae et Evae*,"[8] which would give the work a much earlier date before Christ. Regardless of its

[8] *The Jewish Encyclopedia*, Vol. 8, p. 204. Funk and Wagnalls Company, 1904.

authorship or date, Origen most likely had access to the work while writing his commentaries.

The Life of Adam and Eve contains a dialogue between the devil and Adam that touches on several themes reviewed earlier in the book, such as the devil's presence in heaven prior to his fall, his jealousy of Adam, his refusal to worship Adam, and his banishment from the heavenly realm along with his angels:

> And with a heavy sigh, the devil spake: 'O Adam! all my hostility, envy, and sorrow is for thee, since it is for thee that I have been expelled from my glory, which I possessed in the heavens in the midst of the angels and for thee was I cast out in the earth.' (*12:1-2*)

> And Michael went out and called all the angels saying: 'Worship the image of God as the Lord God hath commanded.' And Michael himself worshipped first; then he called me and said: 'Worship the image of God the Lord.' And I answered, 'I have no (need) to worship Adam.' And since Michael kept urging me to worship, I said to him, 'Why dost thou urge me? I will not worship an inferior and younger being (than I). I am his senior in the Creation, before he was made was I already made. It is his duty to worship me.' (*14:1-3*)

> When the angels, who were under me, heard this, they refused to worship him. And Michael saith, 'Worship the image of God, but if thou wilt not worship him, the Lord God will be wrath with thee.' And I said, 'If He be wrath with me, I will set my seat above the stars of heaven and will be like the Highest.' And God the Lord was wrath with me and

> banished me and my angels from our glory; and on thy account were we expelled from our abodes into this world and hurled on the earth. (*15:1-3; 16:1-2*)[9]

Students of the scriptures will easily recognize that none of the content in these passages is supported in scripture, which is why pseudepigraphal works such as these were not canonized. Just reading its text, I get the impression that something is very wrong with this theology. Such as, why would God, the most holy uncreated Creator whom the angels alone worship, command the angels to bow down and worship man, a created being? The whole story strikes me as bizarre and totally against the character of God. But, I point out this work because it was likely influential to the early church fathers in the development of the story of Lucifer.

The second pseudepigraphal work that may have been influential to Origen and other early church fathers is *Slavonic Enoch*, also known as *II Enoch* or *The Secrets of Enoch*. Similar to *The Life of Adam and Eve*, the date and authorship of *Slavonic Enoch* is unknown, although most scholars believe it had Jewish authorship and was written in the first century.[10] There are two separate passages of interest for this discussion:

> And from the rock I cut off a great fire, and from the fire I created the orders of the incorporeal ten troops of angels, and their weapons are fiery and their raiment a burning flame, and I commanded that each one should stand in his order. And one from out the order of angels, having turned away with the order that was under him, conceived an impossible thought, to place his throne higher than the clouds

---

[9] Charles, R. H., translator. *The Life of Adam and Eve*, The Apocrypha and Pseudepigrapha of the Old Testament, Oxford: Clarendon Press, 1913.
[10] "Second Book of Enoch," Wikipedia, the free online encyclopedia, http://en.wikipedia.org/wiki/II_Enoch, accessed September 11, 2011.

> above the earth, that he might become equal in rank to my power. And I threw him out from the height with his angels, and he was flying in the air continuously above the bottomless. (*II Eno 29:2-4*)

In the passage above, the Lord explained to Enoch how the creation of the earth was accomplished in one week. In the midst of this explanation, the Lord revealed that one of the angels, along with the angels subordinate to him, rebelled and was punished. The second passage provides more detail to this story:

> The devil is the evil spirit of the lower places, as a fugitive he made Sotona from the heavens as his name was Satanail, thus he became different from the angels, but his nature did not change his intelligence as far as his understanding of righteous and sinful things. And he understood his condemnation and the sin which he had sinned before, therefore he conceived thought against Adam, in such form he entered and seduced Eva, but did not touch Adam. (*II Eno 31:4-5*)

The Lord explained to Enoch in this passage that the devil was banished from the heavens, and had previously committed a sin against the Lord. These passages reveal mysteries that are not found in the canonized scriptures, and could have influenced the early church fathers if they considered them reliable accounts of history.

Regardless of whether Origen's interpretations came before or after the passages from *The Life of Adam and Eve* and *Slavonic Enoch*, it is clear that by the middle of the third century, the story of the fall of Lucifer from heaven was fully formed.

St. Jerome's Latin Vulgate Translation

The development of the tradition of the fall of Lucifer, while in full force after the development by Tertullian and Origen, received a major boost when St. Jerome produced the Latin Vulgate translation of the Bible from the end of the fourth century to the turn of the fifth century. With both the Hebrew Old Testament and the Greek Septuagint at his disposal, St. Jerome chose to translate the Hebrew *heilel ben-shachar* and the Greek *heosphoros* of Isaiah 14:12 as *lucifer* in Latin, which means "light-bearer."

But more importantly, St. Jerome perpetuated the story of a fall of Satan as an angel in the commentary on his translation of Isaiah:

> For greater ease of understanding we translated this passage as follows: "How you have fallen from heaven, Lucifer, who arose in the morning." But if we were to render a literal translation from the Hebrew, it would read, "How you have fallen from heaven, howling son of the dawn." Lucifer is also signified with other words. And he who was formerly so glorious that he was compared to a bearer of lightning is now told that he must weep and mourn.[11]

St. Jerome made it clear who he meant by the designation of Lucifer in a number of his writings, such as his letter to Eustochium:

> The devil looks not for unbelievers, for those who are without, whose flesh the Assyrian king roasted in the furnace...Lucifer fell, Lucifer who used to rise at dawn; and he who was bred up in a paradise of

[11] Jerome, Commentary on Isaiah 5.14.12–14, cited and translated in Steven A. McKinion, editor, *Ancient Christian Commentary on Scripture: Old Testament*, volume 10, p. 121. Downers Grove, IL: InterVarsity Press, 2004.

> delight had the well-earned sentence passed upon him, Though thou exalt yourself as the eagle, and though thou set your nest among the stars, thence will I bring you down, says the Lord. For he had said in his heart, I will exalt my throne above the stars of God, and I will be like the Most High. . . The devil fell first...[12]

Thus, in addition to its primary meaning as a poetic song taunting the fall of the king of Babylon, St. Jerome made Lucifer the proper name for the devil prior to his fall from heaven based on the well-established interpretation of that passage's double meaning. Following the lead of the Septuagint translation and Origen's re-translation of the Septuagint, St. Jerome reasoned with his Latin translation of *lucifer* that Isaiah meant to equate the king of Babylon's proud spirit with the planet Venus, or literally, the "light-bearer." But he made it clear that a spiritual entity was being esoterically addressed: the devil.

The Endorsement of St. Augustine

The Latin Vulgate translation became the dominant translation used in the Roman Catholic Church, and thus the story of Lucifer's fall was firmly established as the correct interpretation of Isaiah chapter 14 and Ezekiel chapter 28. This could be made no clearer than by the endorsement of St. Augustine, whom many scholars believe to be the most influential writer of the early church. The Roman Catholic Church holds the interpretations of St. Augustine in the highest of positions among the church fathers. Consider Augustine's view of Isaiah 14:12 and the reference to Lucifer in the Latin Vulgate translation:

> This was written in Isaias: 'How is he fallen from heaven, Lucifer, who did rise in the morning;' and

[12] St. Jerome, *Letter to Eustochium*, 22.4.

> the other passages, which, under the figure of the King of Babylon, were spoken in the same context about the same person or to the same person, and are certainly to be understood of the Devil.[13]

To this day, it is the dominant interpretation in almost every division of the church, including the Roman Catholic Church and Evangelical Christian churches. Without a doubt, the endorsement of St. Augustine of the fall of Lucifer and its acceptance and perpetuation by the Roman Catholic Church resulted in generations of Roman Catholics being taught and believing the tradition of Lucifer the fallen angel.

Summary

Based on the evidence presented thus far, it can be safely stated that, prior to the coming of Jesus Christ, Isaiah 14:12 was in no way connected with Satan in any translation of scripture. With the advent of the New Testament, a new understanding of the passage was introduced by the early church fathers. The key turning point in that new understanding was Luke 10:18, in which Jesus stated that he saw Satan fall from heaven like lightning. Beginning with Justin Martyr and continuing through Origen, the early church fathers connected this statement to Isaiah 14:12 and the interpretation that Lucifer was the name of Satan when he was an angel of heaven before he fell.

After these early church fathers came St. Jerome, who translated the Bible into the Latin Vulgate language. Christian Protestants followed, such as Luther, Tyndale, Coverdale, Rogers, Calvin, Knox, and others, bravely leading believers out of the Dark Ages; a time when the Latin Vulgate translation of the Bible was the only choice for the printed Bible. When the early English Bibles began to be translated, they preserved the Latin word "Lucifer" but

---

[13] St. Augustine, Christian Instruction, 3.37.

applied it only to the "morning star," a reference to the planet Venus. Only the Douay/Rheims English translation, an effort by the Roman Catholic Church to continue its influence upon English-speaking believers attempting to break free from their man-made traditions and false teachings, made reference to Lucifer as the "prince of devils" in its marginal notes to the passage.

The conclusion that I draw is this: the teaching that Lucifer was the name of Satan before a rebellion and fall from heaven is a tradition that was introduced by the Ante-Nicene Church Fathers, codified by St. Jerome, and immortalized by St. Augustine. Origen himself confirmed that the belief that Isaiah 14:12 contained an esoteric reference to Lucifer's fall was only an <u>opinion</u> of the church during his time, not a proven fact. Even so, an army of Latin writers, all adherents of the Roman Catholic Church, espoused the view and made it mainstream for all Christians.

Although Protestants who emerged from the Dark Ages attempted to break free from the interpretation that the devil was being addressed in Isaiah 14:12, as we previously discovered from examining their early translations of the scriptures into English, the influence of the Roman Catholic Church was apparently too ingrained in the minds of believers who emerged from the Reformation. "Lucifer" came to be used as a proper name for Satan in popular literature, and English-reading people accepted the story as fact. But despite the historical progression and the current near-universal acceptance of the story of Lucifer, is it a *valid* interpretation?

5

THE "FALL" OF SATAN

It is now time to explore the context of the key scriptural evidence for the fall of Lucifer. Each of the proof texts used by the early church fathers will be analyzed in depth in the chapters to follow in an effort to discover the truth about whether Satan was once a holy angel who fell. Before the key Old Testament passages in Isaiah and Ezekiel are considered, the New Testament evidence for the fall of Lucifer will be examined.

"I Saw Satan Fall like Lightning from Heaven"

As was discovered in the analysis of the views of the Ante-Nicene fathers, a key verse in the teaching that the devil was once a holy angel in heaven before God's throne is Luke 10:18, the verse in which Jesus stated he saw Satan fall as lightning from heaven. Ignatius, Tertullian, and Origen each made reference to this verse in arguing that the devil was once an angel who rebelled and was cast out of heaven, so it is extremely important to understand the meaning of this passage. Let us examine this verse in its context:

> Then the seventy-two returned with joy, saying, "Lord, even the demons submit to us in your name!" So he said to them, "I saw Satan fall like lightning from heaven. Look, I have given you authority to tread on snakes and scorpions and on the full force of the enemy, and nothing will hurt you." (*Luk 10:17-19*)

This is surely the concrete evidence necessary to prove that Satan was once a holy angel named Lucifer, but rebelled and fell from the heavens right? No less than Jesus himself declared it to be so! But is this single verse in the middle of Luke's gospel truly enough evidence to make that conclusion?

Luke chapter ten begins with Jesus sending 72 disciples, other than the 12 apostles, into the various towns that he would later visit.[1] He gave them specific instructions for their journey and sent them on their way. The passage above records the return of these disciples from their mission, who exclaimed that they exercised authority over demonic spirits in the name of Jesus Christ. At that point, Jesus made his statement regarding Satan's fall.

The traditional interpretation of this passage is that Jesus was making a veiled, esoteric reference to an ancient fall of Lucifer from heaven. According to this interpretation, when Jesus heard the disciples boast about having power over the demons, he felt he should do them one better. Envision Jesus pausing after hearing their excited exclamation, looking up into the sky, and recalling what he saw back in the ancient times. Lucifer, the holy archangel before the throne, was cast out of the heavens for his rebellion and became Satan, the fallen angel. "You think the demons' submission to you is amazing? That's nothing! I actually saw Satan's ancient fall from heaven – he fell so fast it was like lightning!"

---

[1] In some early manuscripts, the number of disciples was recorded as 70.

Growing up, I was taught the traditional view of this passage, and had no reason to doubt it until I did my own research and contemplation on the passage. Thus, every time I would read the passage or hear a Bible teacher make reference to it in the traditional way, I never gave it a second thought. But after careful study, I have concluded that there are two major problems with the traditional interpretation.

First, it assumes a reference to an angel. Look closely at this short verse – where is the reference to an angel? Jesus stated that he saw *satanān* fall, the Greek word for the accuser or the adversary which gradually over time became the proper name of the devil. If Jesus wanted his disciples to know he was referring to the ancient fall of Satan, he could have made it abundantly clear by stating something on the order of, "I once saw the angel Lucifer fall like lightning from the heavens." This would have left no doubt in the mind of the disciples, or of the reader of the text, as to what and to whom Jesus was referring.

Second and most importantly, the traditional interpretation assumes an ancient timeframe when no timeframe other than the immediate context is provided. Based on the belief that the prophetic passages in Isaiah chapter 14 and Ezekiel chapter 28 are referring to Lucifer prior to his fall, Luke 10:18 is assumed to be Jesus' confirmation that he was there and saw the fall of Lucifer. But to import that ancient timeframe into this isolated statement by Jesus is unwarranted.

For example, imagine that I am the manager of a baseball team, and I am having a conversation with my pitcher who was kicked out of the game for throwing a pitch at the opposing team's star player. In reaction to this, members of the opposing team got up off the bench and started to run on the field to stand up for their team's star, but the coaching staff prevented them from going on the field. After the game, my pitcher commented, "Wow, did you see those players on the bench? I was afraid that they were going to come out and attack me!" In response, I smile and say, "Yeah, and you should have seen that player's father up in the stands. He was so mad at you that he bolted from his seat in the back row of the stands all the way to front row! The usher had to hold him back from getting on the field!"

Now, taking this in context, would you be justified in applying my statement to my pitcher to be referring to an incident that happened five years ago instead of the events in the immediate context of the conversation? Of course not! You would understand my explanation of the father running from his seat in the stands toward the field, analogous to Satan in Luke 10:18, to be applied to that same night, not five years ago. But are readers of Luke 10:18 justified in applying an ancient past timeframe to Jesus' statement to the disciples, when the context of the passage was the events that took place during their mission? The application of Jesus' statement in Luke 10:18 to a timeframe in the ancient past results from the desire to use it as a proof text of the story Lucifer' fall, whether or not the context of the passage supports it.

What is the proper interpretation of this passage? These disciples had just returned and exclaimed victory over the demonic spirits when they went preaching the kingdom of God in the authority of the name of Jesus Christ. The most logical timeframe for Jesus' next statement, therefore, is one which coincides with their mission, not a timeframe prior to the Garden of Eden.

While the disciples were on their mission, Jesus saw a sight in the spiritual realm that was both simultaneous and complementary to their experiences with the demons. He saw Satan, the adversary, falling from the heavens to the earth like lightning. Why? Could it have been because Satan was angered that humans, other than Jesus, were displaying power over his kingdom? While the disciples saw only individual evidences of the power of Satan's kingdom being destroyed, Jesus saw a panoramic, spiritual view of the situation. The ruler of the kingdom himself bolted from his place in the atmospheric realm when he saw that his kingdom was being conquered not only by Jesus, but by his disciples.

A Third of the Stars in Heaven

Another proof text for the traditional ancient fall of Lucifer is found in Revelation chapter 12, a highly symbolic passage rendered in the apocalyptic style of writing. The verses most often cited are as follows:

> Now the dragon's tail swept away a third of the stars in heaven and hurled them to the earth. Then the dragon stood before the woman who was about to give birth, so that he might devour her child as soon as it was born.
>
> Then war broke out in heaven: Michael and his angels fought against the dragon, and the dragon and his angels fought back. But the dragon was not strong enough to prevail, so there was no longer any place left in heaven for him and his angels. So that huge dragon — the ancient serpent, the one called the devil and Satan, who deceives the whole world — was thrown down to the earth, and his angels along with him. (*Rev 12:4; 7-9*)

The common practice is, once again, to look at these verses in a vacuum and then draw conclusions from them without considering the context of the entire passage. When the context is properly considered, the passage reveals that at some point in time, a "dragon" caused a third of the "stars in heaven" and hurled them to the ground with his tail. In addition, the passage reveals that at some point in time, there was a battle in the spiritual realm involving Michael and his angels against the dragon and his angels, with the winner being Michael's forces. The dragon and his angels were thrown down to the earth out of heaven. Verse nine makes it clear for the reader that the dragon is the devil or Satan.

The conclusion normally drawn by reading these verses out of context is that the beginning of verse four is a reference to the ancient fall of Lucifer from heaven along with a third of the angels of heaven who rebelled with him. If verse four contains a description of the ancient rebellion of Lucifer and third of the angels of heaven, the author's choice of calling him a dragon instead of an angel named Lucifer is perplexing.

What about the battle in heaven described in verses seven through nine? Surely this is describing a primordial battle between Michael and Lucifer, between the good angels and rebellious angels, just before they were defeated and thrown out of heaven. In order to answer that question, the context of the entire passage must be considered.

The overall setting of Revelation chapter 12 surrounds the birth of Jesus Christ, his ascension, and the persecution of believers, all taking place during the first century. The chapter begins with the description of a woman who is about to give birth to a child:

> Then a great sign appeared in heaven: a woman clothed with the sun, and with the moon under her feet, and on her head was a crown of twelve stars. She was pregnant and was screaming in labor pains, struggling to give birth. (*Rev 12:1-2*)

Verses five and six describe the birth of her son, his ascension to the throne of God, and the flight of the woman to the wilderness for a three and a half year period of protection:

> So the woman gave birth to a son, a male child, who is going to rule over all the nations with an iron rod. Her child was *suddenly caught up to God and to his throne*, and she fled into the wilderness where a place had been prepared for her by God, so she could be taken care of for 1,260 days. (*Rev 12:5-6*)

The woman is a symbol of the remnant believers in Israel, and more specifically, Mary the mother of Jesus, a member of that remnant. Based on the quotations from prophetic passages by John the Revelator, it is clear that the woman's child is Jesus Christ.

So what is the setting for the dragon sweeping a third of the stars from heaven and throwing them to the earth? Based on the symbolic descriptions in these verses, a first century supernatural battle is revealed for the reader rather than an ancient rebellion of Lucifer and his angels. What is the significance, then, of the dragon sweeping a third of the stars of heaven to the ground at this point in the story, just as the woman was to give birth to the Messiah?

Jesus himself declared that Satan had a kingdom at his command, and Paul revealed a hierarchy of evil spirits that Satan apparently has at his command:

> So if Satan too is divided against himself, how will his kingdom stand? I ask you this because you claim that I cast out demons by Beelzebul. (*Luk 11:18*)

> Clothe yourselves with the full armor of God so that you may be able to stand against the schemes of the devil. For our struggle is not against flesh and blood, but against the rulers, against the powers, against the world rulers of this darkness, against the spiritual forces of evil in the heavens. (*Eph 6:11-12*)

Because the context of the Revelation chapter 12 passage in question is spiritual in nature, I believe that Satan recognized that something important was about to happen in the spiritual realm and was marshaling a third of his spiritual kingdom to prepare for the event. Note that the "stars in heaven" he was able to sweep away were hurled to the earth for a specific reason: the woman was about to give birth, and the dragon wanted to devour the child as soon as it was born. In the spiritual realm, Satan wanted his forces fully prepared on all fronts. Eventually, the plan they hatched was for Herod to require all male children two years of age and under to be killed, but the plan was foiled when Joseph was told in a dream to flee to Egypt, which he obeyed.

A Crucial Turning Point

What about the epic angelic war in the heavens described in verses seven through nine which followed this? Again, verses five and six provide the context for this war. The catching up of the male child to God and his throne places these events in the early first century, 40 days after Jesus' resurrection from the dead when he ascended to the right hand of God. There can be no doubt that this is describing his first century ascension, for Mark also wrote that Jesus "was taken up into heaven and sat down at the right hand of God" (Mark 16:19). Verse six appears to employ a small gap of time in the progression of the Revelation chapter 12 narrative, referencing the flight to the wilderness in 66 AD that Jesus told his listeners to be prepared for:

> "But when you see Jerusalem surrounded by armies, then know that its desolation has come near. Then those who are in Judea must flee to the mountains. Those who are inside the city must depart. Those who are out in the country must not enter it, because these are days of vengeance, to fulfill all that is written." (*Luk 21:20-22*)

This places the war in heaven firmly in the first century timeframe. With this context in place, it is not possible to interpret the war as an ancient pre-history battle involving an angel named Lucifer and his rebel angels. What is the correct interpretation? I believe that this passage is describing a very important event in the spiritual realm, a game-changing event: the removal of Satan's access to the throne room of God.

The Old Testament contains two instances in which the adversary, Satan, appeared before the throne of God, apparently in a divine council setting. The first is described in Job chapter one,[2] when Satan and other angelic beings came before the heavenly throne room to make a request to test the Lord's faithful servant, Job:

> Now the day came when the sons of God came to present themselves before the LORD — and Satan also arrived among them. The LORD said to Satan, "Where have you come from?" And Satan answered the LORD, "From roving about on the earth, and from walking back and forth across it." So the LORD said to Satan, "Have you considered my servant Job? There is no one like him on the earth, a pure and upright man, one who fears God and turns away from evil." Then Satan answered the LORD, "Is it for nothing that Job fears God? Have you not made a hedge around him and his household and all that he has on every side? You have blessed the work of his hands, and his livestock have increased in the land. But extend your hand and strike everything he has, and he will no doubt curse you to your face!" So the LORD said to Satan, "All right then, everything he has is in your power. Only do not extend your hand against the man himself!" So Satan went out from the presence of the LORD. (*Job 1:6-12*)

This passage reveals that Satan and the "sons of God," all of which are spiritual entities, had access to the Lord's throne. In addition, Satan had just come from the earth, walking back and forth across it, so he had access to both the earthly and heavenly

[2] There is a similar passage in Job 2:1-7.

realms. Satan convinced the Lord to allow him to test Job, to see if he would remain faithful to the Lord. The final verse in the passage reveals that Satan was actually in the presence of the Lord, face to face with him.

The second instance in the Old Testament describing Satan's presence before God's throne is found in Zechariah chapters two and three.

> Be silent in the LORD's presence, all people everywhere, for he is being moved to action in his holy dwelling place. Next I saw Joshua the high priest standing before the angel of the LORD, with Satan standing at his right hand to accuse him. The LORD said to Satan, "May the LORD rebuke you, Satan! May the LORD, who has chosen Jerusalem, rebuke you! Isn't this man like a burning stick snatched from the fire?" (*Zec 2:13-3:2*)

The Lord, in his holy temple, was visited again by Satan, standing in the Lord's presence to accuse Joshua the high priest. This time, the Lord rebuked the adversary's attempt to accuse Joshua, whom the Lord declared to be a symbolic representation of his servant, the Branch, a reference to his blameless Anointed One – the Messiah (v. 8).

The angelic war in heaven marked the point in history in which Satan and his kingdom of evil spirits were no longer allowed this access to the throne room of God. We know this is the case based upon two important clues in the text. First, the defeat of the dragon, and its consequences:

> But the dragon was not strong enough to prevail, so there was no longer any place left in heaven for him and his angels. So that huge dragon — the ancient serpent, the one called the devil and Satan, who

> deceives the whole world — was thrown down to the earth, and his angels along with him. (*Rev 12:8-9*)

Note that after the defeat, there was “no longer any place left in heaven for him or his angels.” Satan’s role as a member of the divine council, with exclusive access to the presence of the Lord, was eternally revoked! The devil and his angels were then thrown down to the earthly realm, where they were to remain. The second important clue is revealed by a voice in heaven in the next verse:

> Then I heard a loud voice in heaven saying, “The salvation and the power and the kingdom of our God, and the ruling authority of his Christ, have now come, because the accuser of our brothers and sisters, the one who accuses them day and night before our God, has been thrown down.” (*Rev 12:10*)

The voice in heaven provides confirmation that the accuser of the people of God, the adversary, had been thrown down. The one who stood before the Lord and accused them “day and night” was forced out by Michael and his angels. With the ascension of Jesus Christ to the right hand of God to assume the rightful ruling position in his kingdom, there was no longer a place for the accuser to stand. But as the narrative of this powerful chapter continues, we will discover that an enraged Satan would turn his attention to the construction of his evil agenda of persecution and deception.

A Short Time to Attack

Verse 12 records the words of a voice in heaven pronouncing a woe upon the inhabitants of the earth in the first century because the devil knows he only has a little time, and is filled with anger. Seeing that almost 2,000 years have elapsed since that time, why did the voice state that the devil only had a little time? A little time to accomplish what? Based on the context of the passage, there were two pieces of his agenda that he had a short amount of time to accomplish: a spiritual war against the Jewish believing remnant and against a new group of Gentile believers.

First, the devil began a campaign against the Jewish remnant of believers. Think about it: this was an extremely important group of believers responsible for the initial campaign to spread the gospel of the kingdom out from the city of Jerusalem into Judea, Samaria, and eventually to the ends of the earth (Acts 1:8). His best chance to thwart the spreading of the gospel was the desolation of their physical headquarters, which was Jerusalem. Over a roughly three and a half year timeframe, the Roman Empire brought war and devastation to the city of Jerusalem. As previously discussed, the believing remnant of Jews fled into the wilderness in obedience to Jesus' instruction. Verses 14-16 of Revelation chapter 12 provide the details of the devil's attempt to wipe out the believing remnant in Jerusalem, an expansion of what was provided in verse six:

> But the woman was given the two wings of a giant eagle so that she could fly out into the wilderness, to the place God prepared for her, where she is taken care of — away from the presence of the serpent — for a time, times, and half a time. Then the serpent spouted water like a river out of his mouth after the woman in an attempt to sweep her away by a flood, but the earth came to her rescue; the ground opened up and swallowed the river that the dragon had spewed from his mouth. (*Rev 12:14-16*)

The dragon's attempt to destroy the woman was futile, as the Lord God had a place prepared for her in the wilderness. Enraged at the woman and her ability to escape his wrath, the dragon turned his attention to a different group of believers. John the Revelator described them as "the rest of her children:"

> So the dragon became enraged at the woman and went away to make war on the rest of her children, those who keep God's commandments and hold to the testimony about Jesus. (*Rev 12:18*)

The gospel of the kingdom began in the nation of Israel with the 12 apostles, and was taken to the Gentiles in Israel and around the world chiefly by the apostle Paul. Because the devil failed in his initial attempt to attack the believing remnant of Israel, it is only logical to understand "the rest of her children" to be a reference to believing Gentiles. Satan's next move on his grand chessboard was to infiltrate the religious world of the Gentiles.

A study of chapters 13 through 28 of The Acts of the Apostles will reveal the adventures of Paul and his companions as they were commissioned to take the gospel to the Gentile world. Satan was there every step of the way, attacking and hindering Paul's ministry. Over and over, in almost every city, they were met with opposition not only of flesh and blood, but of a spiritual nature. Paul told the believers in Thessalonica that Satan actually blocked his group from coming to them:

> But when we were separated from you, brothers and sisters, for a short time (in presence, not in affection) we became all the more fervent in our great desire to see you in person. For we wanted to come to you (I, Paul, in fact tried again and again) but Satan thwarted us. (*I The 2:17-18*)

In addition to this, Paul revealed in his second letter to the believers in Corinth that Satan sent an agent to attack him physically:

> Therefore, so that I would not become arrogant, a thorn in the flesh was given to me, a messenger of Satan to trouble me — so that I would not become arrogant. I asked the Lord three times about this, that it would depart from me. But he said to me, "My grace is enough for you, for my power is made perfect in weakness." So then, I will boast most gladly about my weaknesses, so that the power of Christ may reside in me. (*II Cor 12:7b-9*)

Having failed in his attempt to stop the spread of the gospel throughout the nations encompassing the Roman Empire, Satan changed his strategy. Instead of fighting against the movement led by the apostles, he began a stealth infiltration campaign in an attempt to merge true Christianity with existing pagan religious practices. Already known for elevation of its Caesars to the status of godhood, Satan was eventually able to successfully merge a false version of Christianity within the constructs of the Roman Empire through the Pontifex Maximus, the Pope, and the Roman Catholic Church. While a full examination of Satan's merging of true Christianity with the religious practices of the Roman Catholic Church is beyond the scope of this book, history confirms that he was successful. Today, the religious mammoth known as the Roman Catholic Church has over a billion adherents to its religious traditions and rituals.

The end of Revelation chapter 12 and the beginning of chapter 13 reveal the engine for Satan's infiltration campaign. Having given up pursuit of the woman to go after the rest of her children who believe the gospel, the dragon is seen standing "on the sand of the seashore" in the final verse of Revelation chapter 12. The next chapter begins with the vision of a blasphemous beast rising up out of the sea, a beast orchestrated by Satan as he stood on the seashore. He then gave the beast his power, throne, and great authority (Rev. 13:2). This beast had the traits of previous Gentile kingdoms – a leopard, bear, and lion – and, along with the false prophet, deceived the entire Gentile world. Thus, the plan of Satan, standing on the seashore of the Gentile nations after leaving the Jewish woman, was to elevate this monstrous beast and provide him with his power and authority to deceive the nations.

Summary

In this chapter, it has been shown that two major proof texts, when taken in the context of the entire passage in which they are found, have nothing to do with an ancient rebellion of an angel named Lucifer. First, it was shown that the fall of Satan from heaven described by Jesus in Luke chapter ten took place in the first century in response to the activities of the 72 disciples, not in the ancient past. Second, it was shown that two passages in Revelation chapter 12 traditionally thought to describe the fall of Lucifer and a third of the angels of heaven, preceded by an angelic war in heaven, actually took place in the first century in response to the birth and ascension of Jesus Christ.

The chapters to follow will tackle the granddaddy of all Lucifer proof texts: Isaiah 14:12 and the surrounding verses. What is the traditional interpretation of the passage, and what are its strengths and weaknesses? Is there an esoteric, spiritual meaning behind Isaiah's words written to the king of Babylon? These questions will be addressed, resulting in what I believe to a shocking and undeniable conclusion.

6

Apotheosis Denied

Several applications of Isaiah's taunt of the king of Babylon have been brought forward over the centuries. This chapter will focus on the most natural of these applications, which involves the king of Babylon who was contemporaneous with the writing of Isaiah's taunt song in chapter 14. The king is taunted because of his desire for "apotheosis," the transference of a mere mortal to the status of a god.

The Context of Isaiah Chapter 14

As we have covered in-depth thus far, the dominant interpretation of Isaiah 14:12-15 is the hidden, spiritual interpretation: that an angel named Lucifer was being addressed. To better understand whether this interpretation is valid, let us first equip ourselves with a firm grasp of the context of the passage.

The Isaiah chapter 14 passage to be considered extends from verse three through verse 21. The chapter begins with the Lord declaring that he will have compassion on his people Israel, and that they will surely be restored to their land after their time of captivity and suffering in Babylon is complete. In anticipation of their eventual freedom, the Lord crafted a poetic taunt through the prophet Isaiah that was to be spoken by the people of Israel to the king of Babylon:

> When the LORD gives you relief from your suffering and anxiety, and from the hard labor which you were made to perform, you will taunt the king of Babylon with these words: (*Isa 14:3-4a*)

Regardless of whether there is a secondary, hidden meaning, any doubt that the king of Babylon is the primary entity to whom the entire passage was addressed has been removed by the Lord's introduction to the taunt. It begins with a declaration that a time of rest and quiet is upon the earth after the Lord had struck down the mighty oppressor not only of Babylon, but of all the nations of the earth. Then, the prophet reveals a song of rejoicing sung by the evergreens and cedars of Lebanon directed to the king of Babylon himself. This song contains an extremely important piece of data about the status of the king of Babylon:

> The evergreens also rejoice over your demise, as do the cedars of Lebanon, singing, 'Since you fell asleep, no woodsman comes up to chop us down!' (*Isa 14:8*)

The personification portrayed by the trees singing their song clearly indicates that we are dealing with Hebrew poetry rather than literal language. We all know that trees do not speak, but in poetry full of hyperbole and metaphors, they can. It is a form of writing that is not meant to be taken literally. This short song by the trees reveals that the king of Babylon to whom this taunt was written would be dead by the time it was spoken. The importance of this piece of information will be fully developed later.

The taunt continues with more information regarding the status of the king of Babylon. The location of his final resting place was beginning to prepare for his entrance:

> Sheol below is stirred up about you, ready to meet you when you arrive. It rouses the spirits of the dead for you, all the former leaders of the earth; it makes all the former kings of the nations rise from their thrones. (*Isa 14:9*)

Sheol is the Hebrew term for "death" or "the grave," the underground world which was regarded as the place where the dead were gathered. The prophet revealed in poetic fashion that all the former leaders of the nations who preceded the king of Babylon in death were waking up and rising from their thrones to greet him when he arrived.

Beginning with verse ten and likely concluding with verse 17, the former kings of the nations deliver the bulk of the taunt message to the king of Babylon, including the key section in verse 12. This means that the content of verses 12-15, which are almost universally assigned to a description of Satan prior to his fall, was delivered by the dead former kings of pagan nations. Their message begins with a declaration that the king of Babylon, though he presumably thought differently while he was alive, was dead just like them:

> All of them respond to you, saying: 'You too have become weak like us! You have become just like us! Your splendor has been brought down to Sheol, as well as the sound of your stringed instruments. You lie on a bed of maggots, with a blanket of worms over you. (*Isa 14:10-11*)

The king of Babylon would lie on a bed of maggots and be covered with a blanket of worms, obviously strong poetic imagery for the state of dead people who are buried in the ground. The pronouncement of the former pagan kings continues:

> Look how you have fallen from the sky, O shining one, son of the dawn! You have been cut down to the ground, O conqueror of the nations! (*Isa 14:12*)

The former pagan kings mock the king of Babylon, exclaiming that he has fallen from his lofty status in the heavens as a shining stellar body; perhaps the planet Venus as it precedes the rising of the sun at dawn. Hearkening back to the pronouncement of the trees which were chopped down before the king of Babylon died, the former pagan kings then declared that he was experiencing a cutting down to the ground. In the next two verses, the former pagan kings elaborate on the prideful thoughts of the king of Babylon prior to his demise:

> You said to yourself, "I will climb up to the sky. Above the stars of El I will set up my throne. I will rule on the mountain of assembly on the remote slopes of Zaphon. I will climb up to the tops of the clouds; I will make myself like the Most High!" (*Isa 14:13-14*)

These two verses detail the pride and arrogance of the king. In poetic form, Isaiah conveyed the idea that the king of Babylon was so proud that he thought he could make himself equal with Most High God. His throne would be above the stars in the heavens, and he would rule on the "remote slopes of Zaphon," or more commonly known as "the sides of the north." In Psalm 48:2, this location was compared to the city of God and Mount Zion, another boast of equality with God. These verses appear to employ Hebrew parallelism, where two sentences make the same point using different words:

> I will climb up to the sky. (*v. 13*) = I will climb up to the tops of the clouds. (*v. 14*)

> Above the stars of El I will set up my throne. I will rule on the mountain of assembly on the remote slopes of Zaphon. (*v. 13*) = I will make myself like the Most High! (*v. 14*)

The section devoted to the former pagan kings ends with a declaration to the king of Babylon about how utterly wrong he was:

> But you were brought down to Sheol, to the remote slopes of the pit. (*Isa 14:15*)

Instead of the high and lofty "remote slopes of Zaphon," his destination was the "remote slopes of the pit," polar opposites of each other. The Hebrew word for the English phrase "remote slopes" in each case is *yerēkāh*, showing that the prophet was using the poetic art of contrast to make an emphatic point. Instead of the magnificent grandeur the king of Babylon imagined for himself, he was sent to the land of the dead, the dark recesses of the pits of Sheol.

The poetic taunt continues with two questions which again mock the fall of the Babylonian king from his powerful stature while living. These questions are probably asked by these same pagan kings as the king of Babylon makes his descent and joins them in Sheol since there is no indication that the speaker has changed:

> Those who see you stare at you, they look at you carefully, thinking: "Is this the man who shook the earth, the one who made kingdoms tremble? Is this the one who made the world like a desert, who ruined its cities, and refused to free his prisoners so they could return home?" (*Isa 14:16-17*)

The activities of the king of Babylon while alive were those of an oppressive tyrant, but now it was time for payback. The man who made the nations tremble in fear, who ruined their cities, and refused to free prisoners so they could return to their homeland, was now powerless in his grave.

After this, the prophet draws another powerful contrast, this time between the resting places of all the kings of the nations and the resting place of the king of Babylon:

> As for all the kings of the nations, all of them lie down in splendor, each in his own tomb. But you have been thrown out of your grave like a shoot that is thrown away. You lie among the slain, among those who have been slashed by the sword, among those headed for the stones of the pit, as if you were a mangled corpse. You will not be buried with them, because you destroyed your land and killed your people. (*Isa 14:18-20a*)

While the kings of the nations were laid to rest in their own splendorous tombs, the king of Babylon was thrown out of his grave. In graphic detail, his death is compared to those who were mangled and slashed. The taunt song of the king of Babylon ends with the fate of his offspring:

> The offspring of the wicked will never be mentioned again. Prepare to execute his sons for the sins their ancestors have committed. They must not rise up and take possession of the earth, or fill the surface of the world with cities. (*Isa 14:20b-21*)

Now that the context has been presented, it is difficult for me to fathom how Satan ever entered the picture in this passage. Satan was only imported into Isaiah chapter 14 after the New Testament was written, and the connection was made between this passage and

Jesus' statement that he saw Satan fall from heaven like lightning. The arguments for the New Testament passages that have been used to prove that Satan is a fallen angel have already been analyzed in their context. Let us now consider whether the esoteric, secondary application of the ancient rebellion of an entity named Lucifer is valid.

Spiritual Applications

In previous chapters, the application of Lucifer the fallen angel to Isaiah 14:12-15 was explored in detail. We learned how the interpretation originated and examined the history of the translation of the key Hebrew words. For purposes of this section, it would be beneficial to briefly revisit the traditional understanding of the spiritual application of Isaiah 14:12-15.

The Hebrew phrase הֵילֵל בֶּן-שָׁחַר is transliterated as *heilel ben-shachar*, and is properly translated into English as "shining one, son of the dawn" or "Howl, son of the dawn." However, the traditional application of this phrase to Satan exists because the Latin translation rendered the Hebrew הֵילֵל as *lucifer*, following the Greek translation of *heosphoros*, both epithets for the planet Venus in their respective languages. Scholars and translators through the centuries believed Isaiah was poetically comparing the king of Babylon to the planet Venus.

Through a series of interpretations by certain early church fathers and influential patron saints of the Roman Catholic Church, Lucifer eventually became known as a proper name for Satan. Using information in Isaiah 14:12-15 and Ezekiel chapter 28, as well as certain passages in the New Testament, a story was built around this entity named Lucifer. He was formerly a beautiful angel in heaven who grew jealous of God's creation of humanity, thought he could exalt himself to a position above God, and convinced one third of the angels of heaven to rebel against God. Because of his pride, Lucifer and his angels were cast from heaven, where he became the archenemy of God known as Satan. To be fair, those who hold this view believe that the primary entity to whom the passage was addressed was the king of Babylon, but that there is a secondary, esoteric application in which we are taken back to the ancient rebellion of Satan.

In recent years, Dr. Michael Heiser, a Christian scholar of ancient languages, has contributed new ideas into the application of Lucifer in Isaiah 14:12-15. Dr. Heiser, in his rough draft of *The Myth That is True*, put forth the idea that the meaning of the Hebrew word *nâchâsh* used in Genesis chapter three to describe the serpent in the Garden of Eden, should not be translated with the English word "snake" or "serpent," but rather with the adjective "shining one." He argued that Eve did not converse with a talking serpent, but rather with a luminous, divine being:

> The word nachash is a very elastic term in Hebrew. It can function as a noun, a verb, or even as an adjective. When nachash functions as a noun it means "snake," and so the traditional translation is possible—but it yields the contradiction with Ezekiel 28 and Isaiah 14 noted above. When nachash serves as a verb it means "to practice divination"…When a verb receives an article attached to it, the action of the verb is then transformed into a person doing the action. Hence the word ha-nachash would then best be translated "the diviner."
>
> The third option—the adjectival meaning of nachash—is the solution to the contradiction problem. When nachash serves as an adjective, its meaning is "shining bronze" or "polished" (as in "shiny"). By adding the definite article to the word, ha-nachash would then quite easily mean "the shining one"…

> What's so significant about translating ha-nachash as "shining one" and not "snake" in Genesis 3? Very simply, "shining one" is the literal meaning of "Lucifer." The name "Lucifer" is actually Latin and comes from the Latin Vulgate translation of the Hebrew Old Testament. In Isaiah 14:12, the Hebrew name of the primeval conspirator against God is "Helel ben-Shachar"— "Shining One, son of the Dawn." Translating ha-nachash as "Shining One" removes the contradiction of seeing a snake vs. a supernatural being in Eden since it provides an explicit parallel between the two passages.[1]

The main disagreement I would have with Dr. Heiser's contention that *nâchâsh* should be translated as an adjective ("shining one") instead of as a noun ("serpent") is that the being in the Garden of Eden is in the New Testament referred to as a serpent. Recalling the events in the Garden of Eden in Genesis chapter three, Paul wrote as follows in his second letter to the Corinthian believers:

> But I am afraid that just as the serpent [*ophin*] deceived Eve by his treachery, your minds may be led astray from a sincere and pure devotion to Christ. (*II Cor 11:3*)

The Greek word transliterated as *ophin*, from *ophis*, is the common Greek word for a snake or serpent, and is used numerous times in the Septuagint Greek translation of the Old Testament as well as the New Testament. In John 3:14, Jesus recalled Moses lifting up a serpent on a pole in the wilderness, a reference to the

---

[1] Heiser, Dr. Michael S. *The Myth That is True: Rediscovering the Cosmic Narrative of the Bible*, Chapter 5, pp. 58-9. Rough draft made available online through contact with the author.

story in Numbers chapter 21 when Moses crafted a brass snake and put it on a pole so that the children of Israel could be healed of a plague. The Greek word for serpent in this verse is *ophin,* and the Septuagint Greek rendering of the passage in Numbers chapter 21 used this same Greek word. Paul referred to the same story in I Corinthians 10:9, and again used the same Greek word.

Another consideration is that if the prophet Isaiah wanted to convey a reference to the serpent in the Garden of Eden in Isaiah 14:12, he could have used the same Hebrew word as was used in that case, *nâchâsh,* instead of *heilel* from either the root form of *hâlal*, or *yalal*. For these reasons, I believe, as Paul confirmed in his letter to the Corinthians, Satan deceived Eve in the Garden of Eden through a serpent, a member of the animal kingdom, not a shining divine being.

Ten Difficulties to Resolve

The arguments against the traditional, spiritual application of this passage to Satan are exhaustive, but have been narrowed down to those enumerated below. Please keep in mind the previous discussion of the context of the passage, Isaiah 14:4-21.

1. *The entire passage was to taunt the king of Babylon, a human being.* The subject of the taunt was addressed as "the man" who shook the earth, and there is no possible way that Satan, a supernatural being, could be considered a man. There is no mention whatsoever of an angel or a spiritual being in the passage.
2. *The king of Babylon clearly died a physical death.* The trees declared the entity had "fallen asleep," a common euphemism for death. In addition, the entity was said to have descended to Sheol, the land of the dead, and had a bed full of maggots and worms, graphic poetic language for the death of a human being. As a supernatural entity, Satan cannot die a physical death, and thus the entire passage

cannot apply to him. Furthermore, Jesus confirmed that spiritual beings such as angels in heaven do not experience death:

> In fact, they can no longer die, because they are equal to angels and are sons of God, since they are sons of the resurrection. (*Luk 20:36*)

3. *Sheol, the land of death and the grave, was never described as the abode of Satan.* The entity addressed in the passage was sent down to the pits of Sheol and greeted by former pagan kings who taunted him. Sheol was never described as the location of Satan's abode. As was discussed in a previous chapter, Satan's abode was either in the heavenly realm (Job chapters one and two) or on the earth (Revelation chapter 12). Though his final destination will be a lake of fire according Revelation chapter 20, that will only occur at the final judgment.
4. *The former pagan kings declare the king of Babylon had become just like them.* Unlike the king of Babylon at his death becoming just like the former pagan kings who had died before him, Satan could never be said to have become weak like the kings of the nations, nor "just like" humans in a state of death. Satan is a supernatural being and could never be compared to a human being in this manner, whether dead or alive.
5. *Heilel ben-shachar is properly translated into English as "shining one, son of the dawn" not Lucifer.* This point has been analyzed in depth, and it should be clear that a proper name was never intended by the prophet in verse 12.
6. *The Hebrew poetic style of writing allows for mere mortals to make claims that they could never actually fulfill.* The argument is often made that the passage must have a spiritual application, because a man could never aspire to do

the things the king of Babylon declared he would accomplish. This argument is fallacious because it fails to recognize the literary style in which the passage was written. The hyperbole and exaggeration used in this passage are common in Hebrew poetry found in Old Testament prophetic books, and thus it was perfectly acceptable for the prophet to assign them to the king of Babylon. Just one example among many can be found in Obadiah, where the Lord addressed the nation of Edom:

> "Your presumptuous heart has deceived you — you who reside in the safety of the rocky cliffs, whose home is high in the mountains. You think to yourself, 'No one can bring me down to the ground!' Even if you were to soar high like an eagle, even if you were to make your nest among the stars, I can bring you down even from there!" says the LORD. (*Oba 1:3b-4*)

The nation of Edom could never soar like an eagle or have a nest in the stars, and yet the Lord stated that he would bring them down from that lofty position. Even Jesus spoke in language of this type:

> And you, Capernaum, will you be exalted to heaven? No, you will be thrown down to Hades! For if the miracles done among you had been done in Sodom, it would have continued to this day. (*Mat 11:23*)

7. *If Lucifer was the wisest of all the angels of heaven prior to his fall, why would he have such an unwise idea that he could become like God?* The five "I will" statements traditionally assigned to Lucifer the angel prior to his fall do not fit the common belief that he was a very wise and

perfect angel. If Lucifer were truly before the throne of God, able to view his power and majesty, how could he come up with the idea that he could rise up against him? Lucifer would have been a being created by this God, so to think he could defeat him is about as unwise an idea as could possibly be conceived.

8. *The Lucifer of tradition was already in heaven.* If "Lucifer" was a beautiful heavenly angel at the throne of God, then why would he declare that he would ascend up to heaven (v. 13)? He was already there.
9. *The Hebrew word transliterated as heilel is found in two other verses in the Old Testament, and in each case is translated as "howl."* If the translation of this Hebrew word had been consistent with the other instances in the Old Testament, there would never have been an English entity named "Lucifer" in this verse, and perhaps never a false connection made to Satan. The context of the passage perfectly supports a "howl" translation, as the king of Babylon was dead just like the other kings and was descending to Sheol – more than enough reason to howl in anguish.
10. *Satan had access to the throne of God, and yet he was cast down to Sheol?* If you find yourself still clinging to the traditional interpretation of this passage, this should clinch the matter. How is it that Satan could have access to the throne room as a member of the divine council as recorded in Job chapters one and two *after being cast into* Sheol? How could he appear before the throne as recorded in Zechariah chapter three? If Lucifer was cast out of heaven and assigned to the pits of Sheol, how could he later reappear in the heavenly realm after that event? The fact is that Satan was not cast down to Sheol, but had access to the throne of God until no room was found for him there – made clear in our examination of Revelation chapter 12.

Summary

The bottom line is that an application of Satan to this passage involves picking and choosing certain verses out of context and ignoring the surrounding verses if they don't support the passage. What results is a mockery of scripture, torturing the text until it gives in and confesses. Consider what biblical scholar and commentator Adam Clarke wrote regarding this very passage in that regard:

> And although the context speaks explicitly concerning Nebuchadnezzar, yet this has been, I know not why, applied to the chief of the fallen angels, who is most incongruously denominated Lucifer, (the bringer of light!) an epithet as common to him as those of Satan and Devil. That the Holy Spirit by his prophets should call this arch-enemy of God and man the light-bringer, would be strange indeed. But the truth is, the text speaks nothing at all concerning Satan nor his fall, nor the occasion of that fall, which many divines have with great confidence deduced from this text. O how necessary it is to understand the literal meaning of Scripture, that preposterous comments may be prevented![2]

The same train of thought is found in *The Popular and Critical Bible Encyclopedia and Scriptural Dictionary* in this entry:

> The application of this passage to Satan, and to the fall of the apostate angels, is one of those gross perversions of Sacred Writ which so extensively obtain, and which are to be traced to a proneness to seek for more in any given passage than it really contains, a disposition to be influenced by sound

[2] Clarke, Adam. Commentary on the Bible, Isaiah 14:12.

> rather than sense, and an implicit faith in received interpretations.[3]

Incongruous, strange, preposterous, gross perversion, and senseless; all apt descriptions of the spiritual application of this passage to Satan.

Two key questions that those who cling to the traditional story of the fall of Lucifer must answer are (1) how could an angel described as being full of wisdom make such an unwise miscalculation to think he could become like the Most High God, and (2) how could Lucifer, being thrown down from heaven and confined in Sheol in the ancient past, be seen later before the throne of God in heaven in Job chapters one and two? In the chapter to follow, a simple and profound application of this misunderstood passage will be provided.

---

[3] Fallows, Samuel (Editor). *The Popular and Critical Bible Encyclopedia and Scriptural Dictionary*, Vol. 2, p. 1082. The Howard-Severance Company (1902).

7

The True Morning Star

Scholars have debated for centuries about exactly what Isaiah had in mind when he cited the taunt of the former pagan kings directed to the king of Babylon in Isaiah 14:12-15. The Hebrew phrase הֵילֵל בֶּן-שָׁחַר, transliterated into English as *heilel ben-shachar* and translated as "shining one, son of the dawn," has captivated their imagination. They insist that Isaiah must have been alluding to a historical biblical figure or some kind of pre-existing myth that the king of Babylon would have known about. This chapter will explore these myths, and conclude with what I believe to be the best interpretation of Isaiah 14:12 that the prophet, through the Holy Spirit, was attempting to convey to the reader.

Historical Figures and Myths

One historical figure that some have attempted to apply to the taunt song is the first king of Babylon, Nimrod. According to Genesis chapter ten, Nimrod had a kingdom in the land of Shinar, where he led the construction of the Tower of Babel. This is the location of ancient Babylon, and Nimrod was its first king. An application to Nimrod fits some of the taunt narrative, namely the five "I will" statements. According to certain ancient sources such as the scroll of *Jasher* and Flavius Josephus' *Antiquities of the Jews*, Nimrod's goal was to build the tower so high that it could reach heaven, which some have said is analogous to the boasts of Isaiah's king of Babylon. Although the best application is to the king of Babylon who was contemporaneous to the writing of Isaiah's taunt song, some would argue that Isaiah meant for it to have a secondary application to Nimrod, Babylon's first king.

The most common myth applied to the king of Babylon is found in the Ugaritic texts, involving a god named Athtar and the "most high god" Baal. According to this myth, Athtar attempted to take the vacant throne of Baal on the summit of Mount Zaphon, but was unsuccessful. One of Athtar's parents promoted him to the throne of Baal, but Athtar admitted his inferiority to Baal and voluntarily descended from the throne of Baal in the heavens to rule over the earth.[1]

There are numerous problems with connecting this myth to Isaiah 14:12-15. First, the name of the entity in the myth is Athtar, not *heilel*. Second, Athtar is the offspring of the gods El and Ahirat, but *heilel* was the son of *shachar*, "the dawn." Third, Athtar admitted his own inferiority in contrast to the entity addressed in Isaiah who boasted of becoming equal with God. Fourth, Athtar actually took the throne of Baal, while the entity addressed in Isaiah never ascended to the heavens to the throne of God. Finally, Athtar voluntarily descended from the throne, but the entity addressed in Isaiah was unceremoniously taken down to the pits of Sheol, the land of the dead. For these reasons, the equating the Ugaritic Athtar to Isaiah 14:12-15 is a desperate and unconvincing endeavor.

An even more untenable comparison is drawn between the Greek myth surrounding Phaëton, which means "shining" in Greek.

---

[1] The story of Athtar can be found in the Ugaritic text KTU 1.6 I 53-65.

As the story goes, Phaëton ascended into heaven to his father Helios and asked to drive his chariot, the sun, for one day. Helios eventually agreed to this, but when the day came, Phaëton was unable to control the fierce horses that drew the chariot because they sensed a weaker hand. Zeus was forced to intervene by striking the runaway chariot with a lightning bolt to stop it, causing Phaëton to plunge into the river Eridanos.[2] After our examination of the context of the Isaiah, clearly any comparison of this myth to the taunt song by the former pagan kings is superficial at best.

A Simple, Profound Interpretation

The most logical understanding of the taunt song by the former pagan kings, written by Isaiah through the Holy Spirit's inspiration, is a criticism of the pagan notion of "postmortal stellar apotheosis" of royalty. As previously explained, apotheosis refers to the exaltation of a mere mortal to the status of a god. Many ancient pagan nations believed that when one of their kings died, he was exalted to the status of a god and made his appearance every night as one of the stars of the heavens.

In fact, such exaltation from the leader of a nation to a god can be found in the capitol of the United States of America, Washington D.C. A massive painting on the inside of the dome of the Capitol Building was completed by Constantino Brumidi in 1865. In this painting, George Washington, the first president of the United States, is depicted with various Roman gods and goddesses such as Minerva, Neptune, Vulcan, and Ceres. The name of the painting is, "The Apotheosis of Washington," in which he sits upon the clouds with a rainbow underneath, draped in royal purple and holding a sword in his left hand.[3]

---

[2] "Phaeton" Wikipedia, The Free Encyclopedia, http://en.wikipedia.org/wiki/Phaeton, accessed May 27, 2011.

[3] "The Apotheosis of Washington" Wikipedia, The Free Encyclopedia, http://en.wikipedia.org/wiki/The_Apotheosis_of_Washington, accessed August 20, 2011.

"The Apotheosis of Washington"[4]

Postmortal stellar apotheosis was greatly desired both by ancient pagan kings and those who revered them. I believe that the purpose of Isaiah chapter 14 was to taunt the aspirations of the king of Babylon to achieve this apotheosis in the afterlife. Through the words of the former pagan kings, Isaiah was taunting the king of Babylon that his dream of apotheosis was going to be denied. This thesis is explained in great detail by its author, Matthias Albani, in a paper entitled, "*The Downfall of Helel, the Son of Dawn: Aspects of Royal Ideology in Isa 14:12-13.*" In his paper, Albani begins with a matter-of-fact declaration of what the passage is not about:

[4] Image accessed on Wikipedia, The Free Encyclopedia at the following address: http://en.wikipedia.org/wiki/File:Apotheosis_of_ George_Washington.jpg

> The Vulgate translates the Hebrew *Helel* as *Lucifer*...According to this tradition Satan belonged primordially to the first light creatures of God and was cast down from heaven because of his arrogant pride. This account became more widespread in Christian theology thanks to Origen, who related Isa 14:12-13 to the Jesus logion of Lk 10:18 by interpreting *Helel* as Satan. The fall of the king of Tyre (Ezek 28:11-19) was interpreted in the same way in patristic literature...As a result, since the Middle Ages *Lucifer* has become a common name for the devil. However, the figure of *Helel* in Isa 14:12 has nothing to do with the devil.[5]

Albani continues with several examples from Canaanite and Egyptian sources regarding the notion of the royal ascendancy to stellar prominence after death. According to Albani:

> In Egypt the king was regarded *inter alia* as "son of Re" who ascends after his death to the sun and to the immortal stars. In light of the designation "son of dawn" it is of particular importance that the deceased Egyptian king is designated as "Morning Star" or is associated with this special star. This occurs, for example, in the pyramid texts: "You ascend to the sky as a star, as the Morning Star"...[6]
>
> With respect to the royal designation "son of dawn" in Isa 14:12 another Pyramidic text is [a] very instructive: 'O king, the sky conceives you with

---

[5] Albani, Matthias, "The Downfall of Helel, the Son of Dawn: Aspects of Royal Ideology in Isa 14:12-13," in Christoph Auffarth and Loren T. Struckenbruck, Editors, *The Fall of the Angels*, p. 62. Koninklijke Brill, NV: Leiden, The Netherlands, 2004.

[6] *Ibid*, pp. 67-8.

> Orion, the dawn-light bears you with Orion. He who lives, lives by the command of the gods, and you live. You will regularly ascend with Orion from the eastern region of the sky, you will regularly descend with Orion from the western region of the sky.'[7]

These clues reveal that ancient Egyptians believed just as these pagan kings did, who taunted the king of Babylon. First, they declare he had become just like them, ushered into Sheol and decomposing in a grave. Then they taunt him as a "shining one, son of the dawn," a reference to the king's desire for postmortal stellar divinity. Note that the sky and the dawn's light were said to conceive the Egyptian king, hence the reference to "son of the dawn." Though the king declared in his heart that he would be in the sky above all the other stars of God, and that he would become like the Most High God, he was brought down to the pits of Sheol.

Albani also points out the hubris of the king of Babylon in that he was not satisfied with the usual place among the stars with the other kings. Instead, he wanted to have equality with the Most High in his postmortal existence since in his mortal existence he occupied the highest position of authority on the earth. His punishment was not merely that he would lie down in Sheol with the other pagan kings, but rather, that he would be cast from his grave like a worthless branch and lie among the slain as if he were a mangled corpse. "Both his postmortal existence and his memory are in this way totally extinguished."[8]

What is profound about Albani's thesis is how it completely supports the royal apotheosis of Jesus Christ which the king of Babylon did not attain. In contrast to the exquisite pride and desire to attain immortality in the stars, the true Son of God proved himself to be superior by his resurrection from the pits of Sheol!

---

[7] *Ibid*, pp. 67-8, 70, quoting from R. O. Faulkner, *The King and the Star-Religion*, p. 158.
[8] *Ibid*, p. 76.

Consider the potent words of Paul in his letter to the Philippians, and note the contrast to the hubris of the king of Babylon and the notion of the postmortal stellar ascendancy of royalty:

> You should have the same attitude toward one another that Christ Jesus had, who though he existed in the form of God did not regard equality with God as something to be grasped, but emptied himself by taking on the form of a slave, by looking like other men, and by sharing in human nature. He humbled himself, by becoming obedient to the point of death — even death on a cross! As a result God exalted him and gave him the name that is above every name, (*Php 2:6-9*)

The king of Babylon desired to escape the fate of mortality by ascending to the heavens in a stellar apotheosis. In contrast, Jesus Christ *accepted* the fate of mortality by *descending from* the heavens to the position of humanity, and allowed himself to suffer death. Unlike the king of Babylon, whose eternal fate was entrapment in Sheol without any royal splendor, Jesus Christ conquered Sheol by his resurrection from the dead and ascended to the right hand of God with the ultimate title of royal splendor – the King of Kings! The Psalmist, whom Peter quoted on his Day of Pentecost address, declared that Jesus Christ went to Sheol, the same location of the king of Babylon, but did not remain there:

> You will not abandon me to Sheol; you will not allow your faithful follower to see the Pit. (*Psa 16:10*)

The pride of the king of Babylon resulted in his punishment, but in contrast, the humility of Jesus Christ to the point of death on a cross – a public spectacle of God's wrath on man's sin – resulted in his exaltation. What a powerful contrast! Albani concluded his thesis as follows:

> The resurrection of Christ brings about a kind of democratization of the royal privilege of a beatific afterlife as believers follow and participate in Christ's way of salvation. 2 Pet 1:16-21 alludes to the transfiguration of Christ on a high mountain where the voice of God declares him as "my son, the beloved." It cannot be by chance that Christ, the beloved son of God, is designated in 2 Pet 1:19 as a "morning star" who rises in the hearts of the believers "until the day dawns."[9]

Albani made a powerful connection to Peter's second epistle, in which Jesus Christ was designated as the morning star rising in the hearts of believers. Not only did Jesus Christ conquer Sheol's power over humanity, but he provided a way for imperfect humanity to share in his accomplishment: repentance toward God and faith in the Lord Jesus Christ. Believers are able to share in Jesus Christ's royal privilege of postmortal apotheosis by becoming heirs with him:

> The Spirit himself bears witness to our spirit that we are God's children. And if children, then heirs (namely, heirs of God and also *fellow heirs with Christ*) — if indeed we suffer with him so we may also be glorified with him. (*Rom 8:16-17*)

> Blessed is the God and Father of our Lord Jesus Christ, who has blessed us with every spiritual blessing in the heavenly realms in Christ. (*Eph 1:3*)

[9] *Ibid*, p. 86.

> His servants will worship him, and they will see his face, and his name will be on their foreheads. Night will be no more, and they will not need the light of a lamp or the light of the sun, because the Lord God will shine on them, and they will reign forever and ever. (*Rev 22:3b-5*)

Summary

The entity addressed in Isaiah 14:12-15 has nothing to with Satan or a former angel named Lucifer, and it is time for Christians to break free from this traditional myth. There is a powerful, profound explanation for the taunt song of the former pagan kings delivered to the king of Babylon upon his descent to the pits of Sheol. Because of the power and wealth experienced during his mortal existence, the king of Babylon was filled with pride.

He proclaimed he was going to experience postmortal stellar apotheosis, a divine status in the heavens that would rival the status of the Most High God. The punishment for his hubris and oppression he dealt during his life was, instead of an ascent to the remote slopes of Mount Zaphon, a descent to the remote sides of the pits of Sheol. While the kings before him were laid down in relative postmortal splendor, he was regarded as a worthless branch that was cast from the grave as a slain, mangled corpse. The accomplishment of Jesus Christ provides a powerful contrast to the king of Babylon, descending from the heavens in humility and experiencing the ultimate postmortal stellar exaltation – our Morning Star!

8

THE ANOINTED CHERUB?

As was previously examined, Tertullian was the first of the Ante-Nicene early church fathers known to express in written form that a song of lament to the king of Tyre was actually directed toward Satan, a fallen angel named Lucifer. He reasoned that, because the king of Tyre was not in the Garden of Eden, only Satan could fulfill the descriptions of the Lord's song of lament. Origen, St. Jerome, and St. Augustine followed Tertullian in assigning the Ezekiel passage to Satan for the same reasons, and the idea was adopted as orthodoxy through the influence of the Roman Catholic Church.

Similar to the taunt song of Isaiah chapter 14 to the king of Babylon, examination of the context and writing style of the author is required in order to understand the proper meaning of the lament song of Ezekiel chapter 28 to the king of Tyre. The key section that has been traditionally applied to Satan consists of verses 12 through 16, in which the prophet related the king of Tyre to events that happened in the Garden of Eden. This section will be thoroughly analyzed to determine the proper interpretation and application.

Adam or the Cherub?

Before undertaking a full examination of the pertinent passages of Ezekiel chapter 28, two rival translations of verses 14 and 16 must be examined. The subject of the Lord's song of lament to the king of Tyre is different based upon which translation is considered, and it has a major impact on the meaning of the passage. Consider the different translations of verse 14 in the KJV and the English translation of the Septuagint (LXX):

> Thou *art* the anointed cherub that covereth; and I have set thee *so*: thou wast upon the holy mountain of God; thou hast walked up and down in the midst of the stones of fire. (*Eze 28:14, KJV*)

> From the day that thou wast created thou wast with the cherub: I set thee on the holy mount of God; thou wast in the midst of the stones of fire. (*Eze 28:14, Brenton LXX*)

Note that in the KJV, the prophet addressed the anointed cherub, telling the cherub that he was on the holy mountain of God, etc. But in the LXX, the prophet addressed the king of Tyre through an unnamed entity that was actually in the Garden of Eden, not the anointed cherub, and that entity was *with* the cherub. Next, consider verse 16:

> By the multitude of thy merchandise they have filled the midst of thee with violence, and thou hast sinned: therefore I will cast thee as profane out of the mountain of God: and I will destroy thee, O covering cherub, from the midst of the stones of fire. (*Eze 28:16, KJV*)

> Of the abundance of thy merchandise thou hast filled thy storehouses with iniquity, and hast sinned: therefore thou hast been cast down wounded from the mount of God, and the cherub has brought thee out of the midst of the stones of fire. (*Eze 28:16, Brenton LXX*)

Similar to verse 14, the KJV features the cherub being addressed, with the Lord threatening to destroy the cherub. But in the LXX, the king of Tyre, through an unnamed entity in the Garden of Eden, is addressed.

Why is there a difference in the translations? The actual Hebrew scriptures used for the KJV translation, the Masoretic Text, agree with the KJV translation in this case. However, for some reason, the translators of the LXX differed in translating the original Hebrew scriptures into the Greek language. Many English translations have followed the LXX translation, agreeing that the prophet was not addressing the cherub in the Garden of Eden, a minor player in the Genesis chapter three narrative, but rather was addressing a more important player in the narrative, namely, the first man Adam. This will be evident when the passage is fully analyzed in its context.

According to modern Bible scholars and translators who followed the LXX translation, there are solid grammatical and exegetical reasons to follow the LXX translation. From a grammatical perspective, the controversy centers around the first sentence of verse 14, which the Masoretic Text renders "thou *art* the anointed cherub that covereth, and I have set thee *so*." Take note that the italicized words are inserted in the English translation and do not appear in the original Hebrew text.

This KJV rendering is problematic because the pronoun "thou" that begins the sentence is in feminine singular form in Hebrew, but in all other cases in the passage under consideration, the king of Tyre is addressed in masculine singular form. Recognizing this problem, the translators of the New English Translation (NET) concluded as follows:

> [I]t is more likely that the form should be repointed as the preposition "with" (see the Septuagint (LXX)). In this case the ruler of Tyre is compared to the first man, not to a cherub. If this emendation is accepted, then the verb "I placed you" belongs with what precedes and concludes the first sentence in the verse.[1]

A proper explanation of this problem involves discussion of grammatical considerations beyond the scope of this book. It is sufficient to state, though, that the LXX and other modern translations are justified in their suggested changes because in all other cases, the king of Tyre was addressed using the masculine form. The use of the feminine form as a pronoun resulted in the KJV insertion of the verb "art" at the beginning of the sentence which does not exist in the Hebrew text. Thus, the KJV also inserted words that are not present in the original language. In the LXX translation, the pronoun "thou" is changed to the preposition "with," resulting in "thou wast with the cherub" in verse 14.

A similar grammatical controversy exists with verse 16, resulting in the anointed cherub being the subject of the Lord's wrath instead of the king of Tyre. Again, according to the translators of the NET Bible:

> The Hebrew text takes the verb as first person and understands "guardian cherub" as a vocative, in apposition to the pronominal suffix on the verb. However, if the emendation in verse 14 (i.e., Ezekiel 28:14a) is accepted (see the note above), then one may follow the Septuagint (LXX) here as well and

[1] Translation Notes of the New English Translation (NET) Bible, Ezekiel 28:14.

> emend the verb to a third person perfect. In this case the subject of the verb is the guardian cherub.[2]

In addition to the grammatical reasons, these changes result in proper exegesis of the passage. Instead of addressing the cherub in the Garden of Eden, a very minor player about whom very little is known from the story recorded in Genesis chapter 3, the prophet addresses the dominant subject of the passage, the king of Tyre, through an unnamed entity in the Garden of Eden. This unnamed entity, which becomes clear with a simple reading of the passage, is the first man Adam who was perfect and without sin in the Garden of Eden, but fell. We will see in the next section why he is the only entity that fits the description.

After detailed study and consideration of the passage, I believe that the various English translations are correct to follow the LXX translators rather than the Masoretic Text. However, while these two different translations result in different understandings of the passage, neither translation supports an application to Satan instead of the king of Tyre. This will be clear in the analysis to follow.

The Context of Ezekiel Chapter 28

The Ezekiel chapter 28 passage to be considered extends from verse one to verse 19, but the controversial section includes verses 12-16, which have traditionally been applied to Satan. Chapter 28 follows two chapters in which the prophet delivers an extensive prophecy of destruction and a lengthy song of lament to the *city* of Tyre, rather than its *leader*.

Chapter 28 begins with the Lord addressing the leader of Tyre personally, followed by a charge to the prophet Ezekiel to deliver a song of lamentation to this prince. First, the Lord's personal address:

---

[2] *Ibid*, Ezekiel 28:16.

> "Son of man, say to the prince of Tyre, 'This is what the sovereign LORD says: 'Your heart is proud and you said, "I am a god; I sit in the seat of gods, in the heart of the seas" — yet you are a man and not a god, though you think you are godlike.'" (*Eze 28:2*)

Similar to the song of taunt to the king of Babylon, the Lord mocked the prince of Tyre regarding his pride and his supposed status as a god. Only in the mind of the prince of Tyre was he a god; in reality, he was only a man.

> Look, you are wiser than Daniel; no secret is hidden from you. By your wisdom and understanding you have gained wealth for yourself; you have amassed gold and silver in your treasuries. By your great skill in trade you have increased your wealth, and your heart is proud because of your wealth. (*Eze 28:3-5*)

The Lord continued to mock the prince of Tyre, stating that he was wiser than the prophet Daniel. The wisdom, wealth, and trading skills of the prince were lauded, but they led to a proud heart and his ultimate downfall. A detailed listing of these traits were chronicled by the prophet in chapter 27, including a list of Tyre's merchandise and trading partners. The Lord continued the taunt with an explanation of the results of his pride:

> Therefore this is what the sovereign LORD says: Because you think you are godlike, I am about to bring foreigners against you, the most terrifying of nations. They will draw their swords against the grandeur made by your wisdom, and they will defile your splendor. They will bring you down to the pit, and you will die violently in the heart of the seas. (Eze 28:6-8)

This pronouncement of judgment by the Lord against the prince of Tyre is a summarized rendition of the entire prophecy against the city of Tyre in chapter 26. In that chapter, the prophet declared that surrounding nations led by King Nebuchadnezzar of Babylon would defeat the city of Tyre. The Lord's pronouncement against the prince of Tyre concluded with a rhetorical question and answer:

> Will you still say, "I am a god," before the one who kills you — though you are a man and not a god — when you are in the power of those who wound you? You will die the death of the uncircumcised by the hand of foreigners; for I have spoken, declares the sovereign LORD. (*Eze 28:9-10*)

Hearkening back to the opening statement by the Lord, in which he quoted the prince of Tyre's declaration that he was a god, the Lord asked if he would still make this declaration when he stood before his Creator – the only true God. The clear answer was that he would not, but instead he would be killed by the foreign invaders and die an unheralded death.

Following this personal address by the Lord to the prince of Tyre, the Lord dictated a song of lament to be given to the king of Tyre. This song utilized a hearkening back to the events of the Garden of Eden, a method used by the prophet elsewhere in his book. The song began by making a series of positive statements about the king of Tyre:

> "Son of man, sing a lament for the king of Tyre, and say to him, "This is what the sovereign LORD says: 'You were the sealer of perfection, full of wisdom, and perfect in beauty.' (*Eze 28:12*)

This compliment mirrors the Lord's initial declaration that the prince of Tyre was full of wisdom and "wiser than Daniel." In addition, the beauty of the city of Tyre was one of its major bragging points in the previous chapter:

> 'O Tyre, you have said, "I am perfectly beautiful." Your borders are in the heart of the seas; your builders have perfected your beauty.' (*Eze 27:3b-4*)

At this point in the song of lament, the Lord began to compare the king of Tyre to an unnamed entity in the Garden of Eden. This narrative will reveal things about Eden and its garden that are not found in the descriptions of Genesis chapters two and three:

> You were in Eden, the garden of God. Every precious stone was your covering, the ruby, topaz, and emerald, the chrysolite, onyx, and jasper, the sapphire, turquoise, and beryl; your settings and mounts were made of gold. On the day you were created they were prepared. (*Eze 28:13*)

The entity to whom the king of Tyre was being compared was in Eden, the Garden of God. Like this entity, the king was bedecked with all types of precious stones, which were mounted in gold – a description befitting royalty. The Lord declared that the precious stones and their settings and mountings were prepared on the day that this entity was created. The song continues:

> I placed you there with an anointed guardian cherub; you were on the holy mountain of God; you walked about amidst fiery stones. (*Eze 28:14*)

More about the unnamed entity to whom the king of Tyre was compared is revealed in this verse. The entity was placed in the Garden of Eden with an anointed cherub who was or guarding it. According to the Genesis account, there were indeed cherubim who were guarding the path to the tree of life after the fall of Adam and Eve:

> He drove out the man, and at the east of the garden of Eden he placed the cherubim and a flaming sword that turned every way to guard the way to the tree of life. (*Gen 3:24, ESV*)

In addition, the unnamed entity was on the holy mountain of God and walked about "stones of fire." Scholars have long debated the meaning of these stones of fire. Some believe them to be a reference to the gemstones listed in verse 13 that glistened like fire, wondering whether they were on the ground in the Garden of Eden so that Adam and Eve could walk upon them. Others give them a spiritual meaning, comparing them to the people of Israel whom the king of Tyre was allowed to walk among.

The best explanation is that in the Garden of Eden, the mountain of God was accessible to this entity, and on this mountain there were stones of fire. In the visions of Ezekiel chapters one and ten, the prophet described the mobile throne of God, which featured fire, gemstones, and cherubim. It is possible, then, that Ezekiel was drawing upon these earlier visions and revealing that God was present on the mountain in the Garden of Eden.

The next verse provides the key clue in identifying the unnamed entity in the Garden of Eden to whom the king of Tyre was compared:

> You were blameless in your behavior from the day you were created, until sin was discovered in you. (*Eze 28:15*)

What entities were in the Garden of Eden which could have been used for comparison to the king of Tyre in this passage? Genesis chapters two and three reveal the following were present:

- Adam
- Eve
- The serpent
- God
- The cherubim

One of these five entities is the one to whom the Lord compared the king of Tyre. God can be eliminated, because he was the one speaking, leaving four possibilities. In verse 15, the entity was described as being blameless until sin was discovered in him. The cherubim can be eliminated, as these are sinless guardian angelic beings around God's throne. This leaves Adam, Eve, and the serpent as the remaining possibilities.

The text in Genesis chapter 3 provides the answer. Only two persons in the Garden of Eden had sin discovered in them: Adam and Eve:

> And the LORD God said, "Who told you that you were naked? Did you eat from the tree that I commanded you not to eat from?" The man said, "The woman whom you gave me, she gave me some fruit from the tree and I ate it." (*Gen 3:11-12*)

Because the king of Tyre was a male, it makes logical sense that the unnamed entity in Ezekiel chapter 28 to whom the king of Tyre was being compared was the first man, Adam. He was created perfect and sinless by God, but sin was discovered in him. The next verse provides confirmation that the Lord was comparing the king of Tyre to the first man Adam:

> In the abundance of your trade you were filled with violence, and you sinned; so I defiled you and banished you from the mountain of God — the guardian cherub expelled you from the midst of the stones of fire. (*Eze 28:16*)

According to the descriptions in Genesis chapters two and three, Adam was not involved in any type of trade in the Garden of Eden, but Ezekiel chapters 26 and 27 go into great detail regarding the trade of the king of Tyre. In drawing the comparison between the king of Tyre and Adam, the Lord first made reference to the sin of Adam (v. 15), and then to the sin of the king of Tyre (v. 16). Although their sins were different, they were both guilty of disobeying the commands of God. The Lord then switched back to the story of Adam, revealing that when he was kicked out of the Garden of Eden, he no longer had access to the mountain of God or the stones of fire (v.16). The guardian cherubim expelled him and his wife and blocked their access:

> So the LORD God expelled him from the orchard in Eden to cultivate the ground from which he had been taken. When he drove the man out, he placed on the eastern side of the orchard in Eden angelic sentries [Hb. *kerubim*] who used the flame of a whirling sword to guard the way to the tree of life. (*Gen 3:23-24*)

The remainder of the song of lament applies only to the king of Tyre, not Adam. The Lord listed four negative characteristics of the king of Tyre and four judgments as a result of those sins:

> Your heart was proud because of your beauty; you corrupted your wisdom on account of your splendor. I threw you down to the ground; I placed you before kings, that they might see you. By the multitude of your iniquities, through the sinfulness of your trade, you desecrated your sanctuaries. So I drew fire out from within you; it consumed you, and I turned you to ashes on the earth before the eyes of all who saw you. All who know you among the peoples are

> shocked at you; you have become terrified and will be no more. (*Eze 28:17-19*)

So, where is Satan in this passage? The traditional application of Satan to this passage is nonexistent when it is viewed in context. Ezekiel used a style of Hebrew writing that employed comparison of current world leaders to well-known passages in Genesis. In this case, the fall of Adam in the Garden of Eden, guarded and then expelled by the cherubim, was used as a metaphor for the fall of the king of Tyre. This technique was used to place the king of Tyre in the Garden of Eden, as if he were so perfect that he was compared to Adam – one who was perfect and sinless – until sin was found in him.

If there is any doubt that Ezekiel was referring only to the king of Tyre in this passage, through comparison to Adam in the Garden of Eden, consider a passage just three chapters later written to Pharaoh, the king of Egypt:

> Consider Assyria, a cedar in Lebanon, with beautiful branches, like a forest giving shade, and extremely tall; (*Eze 31:3*)

> I made it beautiful with its many branches; all the trees of Eden, in the garden of God, envied it. (*Eze 31:9*)

> I made the nations shake at the sound of its fall, when I threw it down to Sheol, along with those who descend to the pit. Then all the trees of Eden, the choicest and the best of Lebanon, all that were well-watered, were comforted in the earth below. (*Eze 31:16*)

> Which of the trees of Eden was like you in majesty and loftiness? You will be brought down with the

> trees of Eden to the lower parts of the earth; you will lie among the uncircumcised, with those killed by the sword! This is what will happen to Pharaoh and all his hordes, declares the sovereign LORD.' (*Eze 31:18*)

Ezekiel called the nation of Assyria a cedar in Lebanon, and then compared it to all the other trees in the Garden of Eden. None of this is literal. Neither Assyria nor Lebanon was a nation at the time of Eden. Assyria was a nation, not a tree. Trees do not have feelings or die and descend to Sheol, the land of the dead.

So, if the land of Assyria could be called a tree in the Garden of Eden, before Assyria even existed, could not the king of Tyre be called a man, or even a cherub for that matter, in the Garden of Eden? The answer is yes, when using the literary technique that was unique to Ezekiel.

One Bizarre Angel

The traditional English translations of Ezekiel 28:12-15 have led to some of the most bizarre theology you will hear spoken in Christian circles. Earlier in this chapter, the differences between the KJV and the LXX translations of verses 14 and 16 with respect to the anointed cherub were presented. But there are even more differences between the translations based on the Masoretic Text compared to the LXX translation.

Notice how the differences in the KJV rendering of the passage in question change the meaning of the following verses in comparison to the contextual examination that was just completed. First, the identity of the being to whom the king of Tyre is compared:

> Thou hast been in Eden the garden of God; Thou art the anointed cherub that covereth; and I have set thee so: thou wast upon the holy mountain of God; thou

> hast walked up and down in the midst of the stones of fire. Thou wast perfect in thy ways from the day that thou wast created, till iniquity was found in thee. (*Eze 28:13a; 14-15 KJV*)

In the KJV, the Lord is addressing a cherub in the Garden of Eden, not the first man Adam. This angelic being was a cherub, anointed of God, and had the privilege of being in the presence of God in the holy mountain. These words are believed to have a spiritual application to Satan because, of course, the king of Tyre could not possibly be compared to a supernatural cherub in the Garden of Eden. Other descriptions of the cherub are in the opening verse of the lament song:

> Son of man, take up a lamentation upon the king of Tyrus, and say unto him, Thus saith the Lord GOD; Thou sealest up the sum, full of wisdom, and perfect in beauty. (*Eze 28:12, KJV*)

So the thought process goes something like this, "*Ok, we have an angel who was perfect in wisdom and beauty, we have a reference to the Garden of Eden, and we have a sinless angel in heaven until it sinned...this must be referring to Lucifer's fall and his transformation into the serpent, Satan!*" This line of reasoning is faulty for two reasons.

First and foremost, Satan was not a cherub in the Garden of Eden; he was described as a serpent, an animal. A serpent cannot be confused with a cherub. In addition, a cherub is a special supernatural creature that covers the throne of God. Exodus chapter 24 describes how the cherubim covered the atonement lid of the ark of the covenant with their wings, where the Lord God resided and spoke with Moses:

> I will meet with you there, and from above the atonement lid, from between the two cherubim that

> are over the ark of the testimony, I will speak with you about all that I will command you for the Israelites. (*Exo 25:22*)

Elsewhere in Ezekiel's own writings, the cherubim are described as having four faces, four wings, and straight legs, and they were part of the mobile throne of the Lord. Was Lucifer really a guardian cherub before he fell, with four faces and four wings? The humorous thing is that Lucifer was supposedly a high-ranking archangel on the level of Michael and Gabriel, and yet he is said to be a cherub in this passage! I guess the fact that a cherub is a type of angelic being is 'close enough' to an archangel to apply the passage to Lucifer.

Second, the cherub did not sin in the story of the Garden of Eden; Adam and Eve sinned. As was discussed previously, the KJV translation demands that the Lord was speaking to a cherub in the Garden of Eden, not Adam, and the result is the bizarre theology of a cherub committing sin in the Garden of Eden. The rendition of the LXX and other modern English translations agrees with the story of Genesis chapter three, in that Adam was the being that sinned while the cherub was a guardian placed in the garden with Adam by God.

The KJV also features the translation of certain words in verse 13 resulting in very strange theology:

> Thou hast been in Eden the garden of God; every precious stone was thy covering, the sardius, topaz, and the diamond, the beryl, the onyx, and the jasper, the sapphire, the emerald, and the carbuncle, and gold: the workmanship of thy tabrets [Hb. *tôph*] and of thy pipes [Hb. *neqeb*] was prepared in thee in the day that thou wast created. (*Eze 28:13, KJV*)

What about all the precious stones with which, according to the KJV, the anointed cherub was covered? It has actually been suggested by some scholars that when Satan lived in the Garden of Eden as a serpent, the ground was covered with jewels, and the serpent Satan lived underground in burrows. Because he was burrowed underground above the jewel-covered ground, he was in a sense "covered" with the precious jewels that were littered above him, all over the ground. Perhaps when he came out of the burrows onto the jewel-covered ground, he was walking among the "stones of fire?"

Is it not more likely that the Lord was referring to the king of Tyre who was decked with precious stones in his royal splendor? 'You were so wealthy! Covered in diamonds, emeralds, and gold!' Isn't this more likely than the ground in the Garden of Eden being littered with jewels, and the devil running around on them and living underneath them in burrows? This is not talking about a serpent living under a ground cover of gems, it is talking about a wealthy king bedecked with precious gemstones.

The instruments mentioned in the KJV, "tabrets" and "pipes," have resulted in an even more peculiar idea regarding the original supposed status of Lucifer in heaven. The Hebrew word *tôph* has two meanings, according to *The Complete Word Study Dictionary*. The first meaning is "a tambourine," which is a small, single-headed hand drum with tiny cymbals around the edge. This was the musical instrument played by Miriam in leading the women in songs of praise and celebration after their deliverance from the Egyptians in the Red Sea. The second meaning of *tôph* is a setting for jewelry: the tiny sockets and their arrangements for the placing of precious stones in jewelry.[3]

Similarly, the Hebrew word *neqeb* has two meanings. The first meaning is a setting or prepared location for receiving precious stones. The second meaning is a pipe or cylinder for conducting something.[4]

---

[3] The Complete WordStudy Dictionary entry for H8596, *tôph*.

[4] *Ibid*, entry for H5345, *neqeb*. Neqeb.

For *tôph*, the KJV and other early English translations rendered the word "tabrets," or a tambourine, but the NET Bible and other modern translations rendered the word "sockets." For *neqeb*, the KJV and other early English translations rendered the word "pipes," but the NET Bible and other modern translations rendered the word "mounts." Now, should we allow the context of this verse to dictate which of these meanings is correct? The context involves a wealthy king and a long list of precious jewels. Which is more likely: that the Lord was referring to the sockets and mounts in which precious jewels are set, or to musical instruments?

Ironically, the word "pipes" in the KJV and other early English translations are actually not even referring to a musical instrument in this passage, but rather the cylinder in which a jewel is mounted. Apparently, someone trying to create an interesting theory about Lucifer read the word "pipes" in English and assumed Ezekiel was referring to the wind instruments, such as a flute or bagpipes, through which air is blown to create music!

Based on this translation, some scholars have actually seriously suggested that before Lucifer fell, he had musical instruments *built into his body*, apparently hanging off of him like limbs. This is where the idea comes from that Lucifer must have been musical in heaven – why else would Lucifer have clarinets and saxophones and oboes hanging off his body?! *Must have been musical, probably the worship leader in heaven*, so the story goes.

The final verses of the passage in the KJV present more exegetical problems for the cherub = Lucifer = Satan theology:

> By the multitude of thy merchandise they have filled the midst of thee with violence, and thou hast sinned: therefore I will cast thee as profane out of the mountain of God: and I will destroy thee, O covering cherub, from the midst of the stones of fire. Thine heart was lifted up because of thy beauty, thou hast corrupted thy wisdom by reason of thy

> brightness: I will cast thee to the ground, I will lay thee before kings, that they may behold thee. Thou hast defiled thy sanctuaries by the multitude of thine iniquities, by the iniquity of thy traffick; therefore will I bring forth a fire from the midst of thee, it shall devour thee, and I will bring thee to ashes upon the earth in the sight of all them that behold thee. All they that know thee among the people shall be astonished at thee: thou shalt be a terror, and never shalt thou be any more. (*Eze 28:16-19, KJV*)

The KJV translation of this passage refers to the cherub having some sort of "merchandise" and "traffick" that led him to sin. What was this cherub doing, peddling gemstones in the Garden of Eden illegally? In what kind of commercial trade would a holy guardian angel of the throne of God have the time or desire to engage? Some might suggest that this instead is referring to the sin of Lucifer in heaven before he fell. Did Lucifer get too wealthy in heaven by engaging in trading activity? Clearly, the king of Tyre was being rebuked because of the pride that arose in his heart due to his abundant merchandise and resulting wealth, not a fallen angel named Lucifer.

Summary

What so often happens with this passage, as well as with the passage in Isaiah chapter 14, is that the casual reader of the Bible tries to prove a theology or point of view regarding the origin of Satan. Instead of careful consideration of the context of the passage and the writing style of the author, the passage is taken in insolation. They see an angelic being (a cherub), a sin committed by a previously sinless being, and a reference to the Garden of Eden, then immediately jump to the erroneous conclusion that this must be describing Lucifer's fall. This author was also guilty of this infraction. But the context of the passage depicts the king of Tyre as arrogant, proud, and corrupted by his wealth. That is what is described in Ezekiel chapter 28, not an ancient story of a fallen angel.

All of the inaccurate interpretations of this passage over the centuries have resulted in distortion of the truth in order to support a tradition. The tradition becomes the focal point, while scripture is compromised to the point of confusion and even deception. Our response must be to cast off the traditions and reexamine the scriptures carefully to discover the true meaning of the passage. Such reexamination is usually not an easy task, because it involves disconnecting oneself from long-held beliefs often taught by teachers that we admire and trust. This was definitely the case for me.

9

The Adversary and His Kingdom

At this point, I anticipate that you are wondering if Satan is not Lucifer, then just who the devil is he? If Lucifer's story is merely a tradition that has been successfully perpetrated upon believers through the Roman Catholic Church, then what can we confidently state about Satan and his origins? Allowing the scriptures to guide, much will be revealed about his characteristics and kingdom.

Satan is identified by various names and titles throughout scripture. In the Old Testament, he was identified in relatively few passages as "adversary" with the definite article, so a proper translation into English would be "the adversary," not a proper name such as Satan. The English translations, however, chose to follow the Old and New Testament transliteration from the Hebrew *śâṭân*, as well as the Greek *satanas*, resulting in the proper name "Satan" throughout both the Old and New Testament.

Satan is identified with many well-known titles in scripture, such as: the devil, the wicked one, the enemy, the serpent, the prince of this world, the god of this world, the dragon, the tempter, and the adversary. Satan is a supernatural being that occupies a place in the spirit realm, holding a powerful evil influence over those who do not follow the Lord Jesus Christ. The first time we are introduced to Satan's spiritual qualities after the account of Genesis chapter three is through an interesting narrative in the first two chapters of Job:

> Now the day came when the sons of God came to present themselves before the LORD — and Satan also arrived among them. (*Job 1:6*)

> Again the day came when the sons of God came to present themselves before the LORD, and Satan also arrived among them to present himself before the LORD. (*Job 2:1*)

In these passages, Satan appeared with the sons of God (angelic beings) before God's throne in a meeting of supernatural beings in the heavenly realm. Just like the angels, Satan is a spiritual being, occupying the unseen, supernatural realm. The New Testament confirms that Satan occupies the spiritual realm, the air below heaven and above the earth:

> And although you were dead in your transgressions and sins, in which you formerly lived according to this world's present path, according to *the ruler of the kingdom of the air, the ruler of the spirit that is now energizing the sons of disobedience*, (*Eph 2:1-2*)

Elsewhere in the New Testament, Jude wrote about an incident that took place at the death of Moses involving Satan and Michael the archangel:

> But even when Michael the archangel was arguing with the devil and debating with him concerning Moses' body, he did not dare to bring a slanderous judgment, but said, "May the Lord rebuke you!" (*Jud 9*)

In the parallel passage from Peter's second epistle, Satan is apparently considered to be a glorious being:

> Brazen and insolent, they are not afraid to insult the glorious ones [Gr. *doxa*], yet even angels, who are much more powerful, do not bring a slanderous judgment against them before the Lord. (*II Pet 2:10b-11*)

It is interesting that the archangel Michael, the highest ranking angel who will announce the return of Jesus Christ at his glorious appearing, had so much respect for the devil that he could not bring a slanderous judgment, or what the KJV rendered "a railing accusation," against him. Why is this? Does the devil outrank Michael in some way? Or was Michael just being a polite archangel?

The argument of Michael and the devil over the body of Moses most likely took place in the spiritual realm. The devil may have thought that Moses was fulfilling the prophecy of Genesis 3:15 as God's chosen seed that would crush his head, and wanted to make certain that Moses' body was destroyed. It appears from this passage that Michael the archangel gave Satan a certain level of respect in refusing to judge Satan, but stating instead, "May the Lord rebuke you."

A Spiritual Kingdom

Satan also has a kingdom of wickedness in the spiritual realm at his command. Jesus himself revealed this truth just after casting the demon out of a man who could not speak and being accused of using Beelzebul, an apparent agent of Satan, to achieve the exorcism:

> But Jesus, realizing their thoughts, said to them, "Every kingdom divided against itself is destroyed, and a divided household falls. So if Satan too is divided against himself, how will his kingdom stand? I ask you this because you claim that I cast out demons by Beelzebul. Now if I cast out demons by Beelzebul, by whom do your sons cast them out? Therefore they will be your judges." (*Luk 11:17-19*)

His kingdom, according to this passage, is made up of demonic spirits. In Paul's epistle to the Ephesian believers, however, Paul expanded upon the entities in Satan's spiritual kingdom:

> For our struggle is not against flesh and blood, but against the rulers [Gr. *archḗs*], against the powers [Gr. *exousías*], against the world rulers [Gr. *kosmokrátōros*] of this darkness, against the spiritual forces of evil [Gr. *pneumatika tēs ponērias*] in the heavens. (*Eph 6:12*)

Where did these hateful beings of the darkness originate? Two key passages cited as a proof text for the fall of angels with Satan have been covered in depth previously, but it is worthwhile to briefly revisit them in this context:

> For if God did not spare the angels who sinned, but threw them into hell and locked them up in chains in

> utter darkness, to be kept until the judgment (*I Pet 2:4*)

> You also know that the angels who did not keep within their proper domain but abandoned their own place of residence, he has kept in eternal chains in utter darkness, locked up for the judgment of the great Day. (*Jud 6*)

These passages are referring to the sin of the Watcher angels, the sons of God in Genesis chapter six which had sexual relations with human women. It is not referring to any ancient fall of angels with Satan, who is unmentioned in both texts. *I Enoch: Book of the Watchers*, referenced earlier in this book, greatly expands upon the fall of the Watcher angels. But that text, as well as the verses above, makes it abundantly clear that these fallen spiritual beings are locked away until the Day of Judgment. Therefore, Satan's current kingdom lacks any activity by these bound fallen angels.

Without any further biblical guidance, my belief is that Satan's kingdom, including Paul's hierarchy in Ephesians 6:12, are made up of different ranks of demonic spirits. No less than the ultimate authority, Jesus Christ, taught that there are different ranks of demons:

> "When an unclean spirit goes out of a person, it passes through waterless places looking for rest but not finding any. Then it says, 'I will return to the home I left.' When it returns, it finds the house swept clean and put in order. Then it goes and brings seven other spirits *more evil than itself*, and they go in and live there, so the last state of that person is worse than the first." (*Luk 11:24-26*)

According to the *Book of the Watchers*, these demonic spirits proceeded from the dead bodies of the offspring resulting from the sinful sexual relations between the Watcher angels and human women. Consider God's explanation for the origin of evil spiritual entities as recorded in the *Book of the Watchers*:

> And now, the giants, who are produced from the spirits and flesh, shall be called evil spirits upon the earth, and on the earth shall be their dwelling. *Evil spirits have proceeded from their bodies*; because they are born from men and from the holy Watchers is their beginning and primal origin; they shall be evil spirits on earth, and evil spirits shall they be called. [As for the spirits of heaven, in heaven shall be their dwelling, but as for the spirits of the earth which were born upon the earth, on the earth shall be their dwelling.] *And the spirits of the giants afflict, oppress, destroy, attack, do battle, and work destruction on the earth, and cause trouble*: they take no food, but nevertheless hunger and thirst, and cause offences. And these spirits shall rise up against the children of men and against the women, *because they have proceeded from them*. (*I Eno 15:8-12*)

According to the pronouncement of God, these evil spirits which issued forth from the giants would be an unseen opposing force against humanity. Thus, they would make a perfect fit for instruments of Satan in his kingdom. If this passage does indeed mark the origin of the demonic spirits, then what about the hierarchy that Jesus referred to in describing the exorcised demonic spirit?

I believe that this hierarchy could be made up of demonic spirits who issued forth from the bodies of the giants, beginning with the original, first-generation offspring of the human women and angels. These spirits would be half-human origin and half-angel origin, and would represent the highest level of demon spirits, the principal rulers (Gr. *archḗs*) in Paul's hierarchy. This Greek word literally means "beginning" and "preeminent ranking," and thus could be referring to the strongest, original demonic spirits.

As the giants themselves began to mate with human women, their half-angel constitution combining with full-human women would result in a spirit with one-quarter supernatural angelic origin. The spirits issuing forth from their bodies at their death would represent a less powerful class of demonic spirits, perhaps the powers (Gr. *exousías*) or rulers of the darkness (Gr. *kosmokrátōros*) in Paul's hierarchy.

As the genetic pool of giants became further watered down with the passage of time, the lowest level of demons, perhaps the unclean spirits who went to bring back seven more wicked spirits to whom Jesus referred, would result from the mating of the lesser giant offspring. These would represent the spiritual forces of evil (Gr. *pneumatika tēs ponērias*) in the heavens in Paul's hierarchy.

Certain other passages have been traditionally understood to refer to evil supernatural beings that are members of Satan's kingdom, but can also be understood as references to spirits commissioned by the Lord to do his will. One such passage is the lying spirit in the mouth of the false prophets of Ahab:

> Micaiah said, "That being the case, hear the word of the LORD. I saw the LORD sitting on his throne, with all the heavenly assembly standing on his right and on his left. The LORD said, 'Who will deceive Ahab, so he will attack Ramoth Gilead and die there?' One said this and another that. Then a spirit stepped forward and stood before the LORD. He said, 'I will deceive him.' The LORD asked him, 'How?' He replied, 'I will go out and be a lying spirit in the mouths of all his prophets.' The LORD said, 'Deceive and overpower him. Go out and do as you have proposed.' So now, look, the LORD has

> placed a lying spirit in the mouths of all these prophets of yours; but the LORD has decreed disaster for you." (*I Kin 22:19*)

Not only did this lying spirit come from the Lord's throne to deceive Ahab, but the idea to deceive Ahab originated with the Lord himself. Only after asking one of the members of his divine council to deceive Ahab so that he could be killed in battle did this spiritual being step forward. There is no indication that this was an evil spirit in league with Satan; on the contrary, the spirit was standing before the throne of the Lord and obeying his commands, similar to the sons of God in Job chapters one and two.

A second passage of scripture often cited as evidence of Satan's kingdom involve two spiritual entities mentioned by an angel, believed to be Gabriel, who brought a prophecy of the future to Daniel:

> Then he said to me, "Don't be afraid, Daniel, for from the very first day you applied your mind to understand and to humble yourself before your God, your words were heard. I have come in response to your words. However, the prince of the kingdom of Persia was opposing me for twenty-one days. But Michael, one of the leading princes, came to help me, because I was left there with the kings of Persia."
>
> He said, "Do you know why I have come to you? Now I am about to return to engage in battle with the prince of Persia. When I go, the prince of Greece is coming. However, I will first tell you what is written in a dependable book. (There is no one who strengthens me against these princes, except Michael your prince." (*Dan 10:12-13; 20-21*)

While it is clear from this passage that the princes of Persia and Greece were battling against the archangel Michael (the prince of Israel) and Gabriel, it does not necessarily follow that the princes of Persia and Greece were evil spirits. A somewhat obscure passage in the book of Deuteronomy may shed light on this:

> When the Most High divided the nations, when he separated the sons of Adam, *he set the bounds of the nations according to the number of the angels of God*. And his people Jacob became the portion of the Lord, Israel was the line of his inheritance. (*Deu 32:8-9 Brenton LXX*)

This passage, as rendered in the Septuagint (LXX) Greek translation above, differs from the Masoretic Text which states that the bounds of the nations were set by God according to the number of the "sons of Israel." Besides really making no sense, the rendition found in the Masoretic Text is not considered to be authentic because earlier witnesses such as the LXX and Dead Sea Scrolls render the phrase as either "angels of God" or "sons of God." For more on this topic outside the scope of this book, please consult the work of Dr. Michael S. Heiser titled "*Deuteronomy 32:8 and the Sons of God.*"[1]

The idea here is that each nation or kingdom that rises in the earth has a prince angel that represents them. While that nation or kingdom is in power, their prince angel is also in power. Note that Michael, the prince of Israel, was doing battle with the prince of Persia, the kingdom that was in power at the time. The prince of Greece, which was the next kingdom to rise to prominence after Persia, was the next prince coming after Gabriel. None of the angelic princes are said to be associated with Satan, and there is no need for them to be. The Lord God is the one who set up the nations

[1] Heiser, Dr. Michael S. "Deuteronomy 32:8 and the Sons of God." *Bibliotheca Sacra*, volume 158, pp. 52-74.

in this manner, and the divine heavenly council that surrounded his throne was most likely made up of these prince angelic beings (the sons of God,) none of whom are described as having evil dispositions.

What about the verses that state the devil has "angels," such as Matthew 25:41 and Revelation 12:7-9? These passages are most likely referring to demon spirits, messengers of Satan, which is the primary definition of the Greek word *ággelos*. A spirit of this nature was sent to trouble the apostle Paul:

> Therefore, so that I would not become arrogant, a thorn in the flesh was given to me, a messenger [Gr. *ággelos*] of Satan to trouble me — so that I would not become arrogant. I asked the Lord three times about this, that it would depart from me. (*II Cor 12:7b-8*)

Certainly the Watcher angels who sinned, the sons of God referred to in Genesis chapter six, would be considered angels of the devil because they sinned and are presently locked in Tartarus. Their final place of judgment will be the lake of fire, along with Satan and his horde of demon spirits, who issued forth from the giant offspring of the Watcher angels.

Angel Genetics

Many object to the possibility of angels having sexual relations with human beings, and thus dismiss the teaching that demon spirits issued forth from the offspring of angels and humans. The primary objection is based upon one scripture taken completely out of context, but the secondary objection is based upon both a misunderstanding of the nature of angels and the fact that it is too much for their minds to accept. How could an angel, a spiritual being, have sexual relations with a human being? How could angels pass the necessary genetic material into a woman so that she could conceive a child?

While these concerns may seem to be insurmountable to the human mind, they are not. First, scripture is clear that angels did indeed have sexual relations with human women. The passage is found in Genesis chapter six:

> When humankind began to multiply on the face of the earth, and daughters were born to them, the sons of God saw that the daughters of humankind were beautiful. Thus they took wives for themselves from any they chose. (*Gen 6:1-2*)

As previously examined, the "sons of God" or *bên 'ĕlōhiym* in Hebrew, are supernatural beings that appeared before the throne of God in heaven. But note that these sons of God left the heavenly realm in order to mate with human women. They came to earth and made a choice, in the earthly realm, to commit sin against their nature. Jude recognized this important distinction in his short but powerful epistle:

> You also know that the angels who did not keep within their proper domain but abandoned their own place of residence [Gr. *oikētḗrion*], he has kept in eternal chains in utter darkness, locked up for the judgment of the great Day. So also Sodom and Gomorrah and the neighboring towns, since they indulged in sexual immorality [Gr. *ekporneusasai*] and pursued unnatural desire [Gr. *sarkos heteras*] <u>in a way similar to these angels</u>, are now displayed as an example by suffering the punishment of eternal fire. (*Jud 6-7*)

This passage contains important clues in understanding angel genetics. First, note Jude's use of the Greek word *oikētḗrion* to describe the place of habitation that the angels abandoned. This word is used in only one other place in the New Testament, and that is Paul's second epistle to the Corinthians:

> For we know that if our earthly house, the tent we live in, is dismantled, we have a building from God, a house not built by human hands, that is eternal in the heavens. For in this earthly house we groan, because we desire to put on our heavenly dwelling [Gr. *oikētḗrion*], (*I Cor 5:1-2*)

In this verse, Paul used *oikētḗrion* to describe the supernatural resurrection body of the Christian in the heavenly realm. In the same way, the angels who did not keep their proper domain abandoned their *oikētḗrion* to commit their sinful acts. They abandoned their immortal, supernatural heavenly bodies to gain the ability to participate in procreation – a pursuit only necessary in the mortal realm.

The second important clue from the Jude passage is the type of sin committed by the angels. Verse seven reveals that the inhabitants of Sodom and Gomorrah engaged in acts of sexual immorality *similar to that of the angels*. It could not be made any clearer that the angels committed acts of sexual immorality than Jude made it in this passage. The Greek word used by Jude was *ekporneusasai*, from which the English word pornography is derived, and means any act of fornication or lewdness. It was used in no other passage in the New Testament, but was used twice in the LXX Greek Old Testament translation. One of those instances was the incident involving Tamar's act of deception and prostitution with Judah:

> And it came to pass after three months, that it was told Judas, saying, Thamar thy daughter-in-law has grievously played the harlot, and behold she is with

> child by whoredom [Gr. *ekporneúo*]; and Judas said, Bring her out, and let her be burnt. (*Gen 38:24, Brenton LXX*)

This is the kind of immoral act committed by the angels in Genesis 6:1-4. A third clue from the passage in Jude is that the angels pursued "unnatural desire" or *sarkos heteras* in Greek, which literally means "different flesh" or "foreign flesh." This indicates that it was against their God-given nature to pursue sexual desires with human women, just as the Sodomite's unnatural sexual pursuit of the each other was against their God-given nature.

Such bizarre stories involving supernatural and natural beings engaging in acts of a sexual nature can cause the mind to reel. *How* can angels do this? I believe this confusion is the result of a misunderstanding of the *nature* of angels when they exit the immortal, heavenly realm and enter the mortal, earthly domain. Remember, Jude indicated that the angels put off their heavenly *oikētérion* in order to take part in the acts of sexual immorality. When angels enter the earthly realm, they do not look like angels – they look like humans and take part in activities in which humans take part.

What activities? Well, how about eating food? That's right, angels ate food with Abraham. When the Lord visited Abraham to announce that Sarah would have a child and also to inform him of the destruction of Sodom, two angels accompanied him:

> Abraham then took some curds and milk, along with the calf that had been prepared, and placed the food before them. They ate while he was standing near them under a tree. (*Gen 18:8*)

Why would angels need to eat food? What happens to the food once it is swallowed? Do supernatural beings possess digestive systems, and does the food eventually become waste? Those who question how angels could have a reproductive system and genetic material when they exit the immortal realm and enter the earthly realm should also have a problem with a digestive system.

One passage that indisputably confirms the possibility for an angel to take on the normal appearance of a human being is found in the epistle to the Hebrews:

> Do not neglect hospitality, because through it some have entertained angels without knowing it. (*Heb 13:2*)

If someone wrote a letter to you today with this advice, you would probably think they were losing their mind. "Ok, so you think angels are walking around my town?" But the author of the epistle to the Hebrews was not losing his mind; he was inspired by the Holy Spirit, and apparently such an idea was considered completely within the realm of reason to both him and his audience. Angels are able to look exactly like a human being when they enter this realm, so much so that human beings sometimes entertain angels without knowing they are angels.

Consider the story of the two angels who visited Lot in the city of Sodom prior to its destruction. The lust possessed by the Sodomites was so strong that they wanted to have sexual relations with the angels that accompanied Lot:

> The two angels came to Sodom in the evening while Lot was sitting in the city's gateway. When Lot saw them, he got up to meet them and bowed down with his face toward the ground. He said, "Here, my lords, please turn aside to your servant's house. Stay the night and wash your feet. Then you can be on your way early in the morning." "No," they replied, "we'll spend the night in the town square." But he urged them persistently, so they turned aside with

> him and entered his house. He prepared a feast for them, including bread baked without yeast, and they ate. Before they could lie down to sleep, all the men — both young and old, from every part of the city of Sodom — surrounded the house. They shouted to Lot, "Where are the men who came to you tonight? Bring them out to us so we can have sex with them!" (*Gen 19:1-5*)

The Sodomites apparently didn't notice any strange distinguishing features about these men to indicate that they were angels or that would be lacking the genetic tools necessary to engage in sexual activity.

The passage commonly cited as a proof text against the possibility of angels having sexual relations with humans is found in Matthew chapter 22. Certain Sadducees confronted Jesus with a trick question about the resurrection of the dead, a concept they did not support. The question involved a woman who was the wife of seven brothers, all of whom died. They desired to know whose wife she would be in the resurrected realm since she had seven husbands in the earthly realm, and was widowed seven times. Jesus' answer made reference to the state of angels in heaven:

> Jesus answered them, "You are deceived, because you don't know the scriptures or the power of God. For in the resurrection they neither marry nor are given in marriage, but are like angels in heaven." (*Mat 22:29-30*)

Jesus in this passage simply revealed that angels in heaven do not enter into marriage with each other. He stated nothing about whether angels possess the equipment or ability to have sexual relations, or what physical activities angels are capable of in the earthly domain. Taken in context, Jesus' answer addressed whether the bonds of marriage are recognized in the resurrection realm, not whether angels can have sexual relations when they take on the form of humans in the earthly domain. A passage in the *Book of the Watchers* related to the sin of the Watcher angels provides additional clues on this topic:

> Wherefore *have ye left the high, holy, and eternal heaven*, and lain with women, and *defiled yourselves* with the daughters of men and taken to yourselves wives, and *done like the children of earth*, and begotten giants (as your) sons?
>
> But *you were formerly spiritual, living the eternal life, and immortal* for all generations of the world. And therefore I have not appointed wives for you; for as for the spiritual ones of the heaven, in heaven is their dwelling. (*I Eno 15:4, 7*)

Notice that the Watcher angels who sinned, according to the Lord God, left the heavenly realm and engaged in acts that were only meant for humans. When they made the choice to leave the heavenly realm and commit the sinful acts, they lost some of their supernatural qualities. Just as Jesus indicated in his response to the Sadducees, angels had not been appointed to have wives and marry. Why? *Because heaven is an eternal, immortal existence for spiritual beings, and procreation is not necessary.* When the Watcher angels made the choice to take wives upon the earth, they forfeited their eternal, immortal existence.

Summary

The scriptures are full of mysterious and difficult to understand concepts regarding the origin of Satan's kingdom. Many times, in order to develop a theology about which we can "feel good," the truth is compromised. We must follow what the scriptures state regardless how unbelievable or far-fetched they may seem to be.

As has been shown in this chapter, Satan has a kingdom at his disposal. This kingdom is made up of different rankings of demonic spiritual entities, against which Paul stated the Christian must battle. Paul listed a full-pronged hierarchy of evil entities, which may have originated from the disembodied spirits of the giants.

As for the sin of the Watcher angels to produce these giants, there is solid scriptural proof that angels took on flesh and had sexual relations with human women. They introduced a new class of spiritual beings, demons, who have tormented humanity ever since. By committing this sin, they forfeited their immortal state and incurred a terrible sentence from the Lord.

The chapters to follow develop the roles, methods, and future agenda of Satan. In addition, I will present what I believe to be the best scriptural case for the origin of Satan.

10

THE ADVERSARY'S ORIGIN AND FUTURE

It may seem strange to be addressing the true origin of Satan this far into the book. But the goal of the preceding chapters was to present the weakness of the tradition of Lucifer so that the truth about Satan's origin could be established. The preceding chapter examined the origin of the members of Satan's kingdom, and now we will explore the origin of Satan himself, as well as his roles, methods, and future agenda.

The Origin of Satan

Absent the traditional explanation of the fallen angel Lucifer, there are very few scriptures that refer to the origin of Satan. But those scriptures provide just enough clues to develop a defendable position. The first passage is in John's gospel, where Jesus addressed a group of Jews who had up to that point believed in his teaching. By the time Jesus was finished challenging them, they had picked up stones to kill him:

> You people are from your father the devil, and you want to do what your father desires. *He was a murderer from the beginning*, and does not uphold the truth, because there is no truth in him. Whenever he lies, he speaks according to his own nature, because he is a liar and the father of lies. (*Joh 8:44*)

The first clue about the origin of Satan is that he was "a murderer from the beginning." To what beginning was Jesus referring? The beginning of time? The beginning of Satan as a created being? Perhaps it is the same "beginning" in the first two verses of this same gospel:

> In the beginning was the Word, and the Word was with God, and the Word was fully God. The Word was with God in the beginning. (*Joh 1:1-2*)

This beginning is, of course, the same beginning found in Genesis chapter one: the creation of the heavens and the earth. If this is an accurate understanding, then Satan's origin was within the timeframe of the creation along with the animals and Adam. Note that Jesus gave no indication that Satan was at one time a loyal, holy angel who later rebelled. No, "he was a murderer from the beginning."

The same author penned another passage which provides an even stronger clue about the origin of Satan. In his first epistle, John wrote as follows:

> The one who practices sin is of the devil, because *the devil has been sinning from the beginning*. For this purpose the Son of God was revealed: to destroy the works of the devil. (*I Joh 3:8*)

This time, John reveals that the devil has been sinning "from the beginning." There is no wiggle room in this statement to squeeze in a holy angel who fell into sin, unless you take "the beginning" back further than the beginning recorded in scripture. That the devil has been evil from the beginning is clear from these two passages. If he was sinning from the beginning, how could it be said that he was holy and upright *before* the beginning? There is no 'before' the beginning. The beginning is the beginning.

There is evidence in Job chapter 40 that angelic beings were present during some part of the creation:

> "Where were you when I laid the foundation of the earth? Tell me, if you possess understanding! Who set its measurements — if you know — or who stretched a measuring line across it? On what were its bases set, or who laid its cornerstone — when the morning stars sang in chorus, and all the sons of God shouted for joy?" (*Job 38:4-7*)

This may have been when Satan was created, because the "sons of God" are spiritual entities with whom Satan appeared before the throne of the Lord as described in Job chapters one and two. Thus, it is possible that Satan was also created at this time and witnessed the creation. However, we cannot be certain about anything other than the fact that Satan was called a sinner, liar, and murderer from "the beginning."

If there existed a clear, undeniable teaching elsewhere in scripture that Satan was originally a holy angel who later rebelled, the description of Satan as a murderer, liar, and sinner from the beginning could be understood as a reference to his *recorded activities* in the early chapters of Genesis. But in the absence of a clear teaching to the contrary, we must understand the words of Jesus and John to be a description of Satan as he was created from his beginning – the moment he was created.

Recall the question asked in the opening sections of this book about the hostility established by the Lord between the serpent and the seed of the woman. Was there previously no hostility between the serpent, Satan, and Jesus Christ, the prophetic seed of the woman?

It was in the Garden of Eden at the fall of Adam and Eve that the adversary first manifested his evil disposition as a murderer and a liar, deceiving Eve and ushering mortality into a world which had not yet experienced death. After this first recorded act of evil committed by Satan, God established hostility between Satan and all humanity, including Jesus Christ, the only sinless representative of humanity.

To Destroy the Works of the Devil

There is another subtle but powerful consideration of the origin of Satan as an evil being from the beginning based on what the New Testament writers revealed about the primary reason Jesus Christ took part in humanity. Consider these passages:

> Therefore, since the children share in flesh and blood, he likewise shared in their humanity, *so that through death he could destroy the one who holds the power of death (that is, the devil)*, and set free those who were held in slavery all their lives by their fear of death. (*Heb 2:14-15*)

> The one who practices sin is of the devil, because the devil has been sinning from the beginning. For this purpose the Son of God was revealed: *to destroy the works of the devil*. (*I Joh 3:8*)

According to the italicized phrases within these passages, Jesus took part in humanity, or was revealed, to destroy the devil and his works. Why was the devil described as the one who holds the power of death? Because he deceived humanity and caused them to disobey God's single command in the Garden of Eden, he was responsible for humanity's death sentence. He held the power of death, because the payment due for sin is death. But Jesus Christ removed from the equation what the author of Hebrews called "the fear of death," and what the apostle Paul in his first letter to the believers in Corinth called "the sting of death," through taking part in humanity and experiencing death as the only sinless person.

What does this have to do with the origin of Satan? Jesus Christ became a human being with a mission to die and redeem humanity. But what if a fallen angel named Lucifer had never rebelled under the traditional understanding? If Lucifer would not have rebelled out of his own free will, then God would have been required to wait around for one of his holy angels to get the crazy idea to rebel and try to usurp his throne; but what if that never happened? If this would not have happened, then Jesus Christ never would have been needed to redeem humanity. Thus, the existence of Jesus Christ in human form, and the plan of God to redeem mankind, was totally dependent on whether or not one of his holy angels would rebel.

One might reply, "Well, God knew that Lucifer would rebel, and so it was in his plan to send Jesus Christ when that happened." The question then arises as to why God would knowingly create a holy angel that would rebel if he already knew that Jesus Christ was going to be in the plan to redeem humanity. Why not just skip the step of creating the holy angel who would rebel, and instead create an entity who would serve the purpose of testing the loyalty of humanity?

Rather than depending on one of his free-will creatures to rebel and *become* this being, it is my contention that God, according to his sovereign purpose and will, created a being that would fulfill these roles from the beginning of his creation. Such a declaration might cause you to cringe, like you were experiencing fingernails scraping on a chalkboard. But it cannot be denied, based on scripture, that God has a use for Satan and allows him to exist.

The mysteries of God's plan of salvation were not revealed to Satan from the beginning:

> And to enlighten everyone about God's secret plan — *a secret that has been hidden for ages in God* who has created all things. The purpose of this enlightenment is that through the church the multifaceted wisdom of God should *now be disclosed to the rulers and the authorities in the heavenly realms*. (*Eph 3:9-10*)

God had a secret plan that, beginning with the establishment of the first century believing remnant, was revealed to the spiritual forces, which would include Satan. God hid this plan throughout the ages, but revealed it through the death and resurrection of Jesus Christ. The questions regarding the origin of evil that arise as a result of this position will be addressed before this book is complete.

The Gap Theory?

Another popular belief about the origin of Satan is referred to as "The Gap Theory," which is an attempt to fit a period of time between Genesis 1:1 and 1:2 when the earth became void after a time of being inhabited by a pre-Adamic race and perhaps dinosaurs. The thought is that perhaps Lucifer fell during this period of time and because of this, there was a judgment upon the earth that existed at that time.

A simplified version of this teaching is represented in the following excerpt from a newsletter received by the author from Elijah's Mantle, the same ministry that was quoted in the first chapter regarding the story of Lucifer in heaven. A month after receiving that newsletter, I received another which continued the story, this time carefully mixing in elements of The Gap Theory to help explain Lucifer's rebellion:

> Remember when we questioned the discrepancy in the creation account? Genesis 1:1 describes creation in a perfect complete state. The word create in Hebrew is the word "Bara" which characterizes a perfectly organized and complete creation. Genesis 1:2 describes the earth without form and void and darkness was upon the deep. Now, that does not sound like a creation in a perfect state, does it? Also in Genesis 1:2, the phrase "was without form and void" in Hebrew is "tohu va vohu hayah" which actually means "BECAME without form and void" So...it is safe to deduce that something happened to change it from its perfect created state to "BECOME" void and without form. Something cataclysmic had to occur to bring about such total devastation. Could that event have been the casting of Lucifer to earth? What we do know is that Lucifer eventually shows up in the Garden of Eden.
>
> The pieces and parts are starting to fall into place. What happens next is chronicled in Genesis starting in Gen 1:2. God RECREATES the earth. This certainly can explain a lot of the question and debate surrounding the age of the earth and existence of dinosaurs in contrast to the apparent six thousand year history of man described in the Bible...[1]

The excerpt explains that a "cataclysmic" event resulting in devastation to the earth, such that it had to be "recreated," must be

---

[1] Excerpt used by permission from Bob Gesing, Elijah's Mantle Ministries, September 2011.

inserted between Genesis 1:1 and 1:2. A passage of scripture that is used to support the idea of cataclysm and recreation of the earth between the opening two verses of Genesis is found in Jeremiah chapter four. Jeremiah 4:23 features the same Hebrew phrase as Genesis 1:2, "without form and void," in the KJV. Because of this, some have made a connection between the two verses:

> I beheld the earth, and, lo, it was without form, and void; and the heavens, and they had no light. (*Jer 4:23, KJV*)

This is another example of taking verses in a poetic passage of a prophetic book and building an entire teaching around them, just like building a theology about a fallen angel named Lucifer out of Isaiah 14:12-15, without giving due attention to the context. There is no pre-Adamic judgment mentioned in Genesis chapter one, and if Jeremiah chapter four is not referring to the time between Genesis 1:1 and 1:2, then there was no pre-Adamic race, no pre-Adamic cities, and no pre-Adamic animals. And if so, Satan's beginning has to be at his creation with the rest of God's creation.

The passage of Jeremiah chapter four in question is a prophecy of great destruction from the north on Judah and Jerusalem:

> The LORD said, "Announce this in Judah and proclaim it in Jerusalem: 'Sound the trumpet throughout the land!'...For I am about to bring disaster out of the north. It will bring great destruction." (*Jer 4:5a-6b*)

First, the Lord makes it clear that the entire passage concerns a coming destruction in the future, not the ancient past. Second, the Lord declares that the judgment will involve Judah and Jerusalem, not the entire earth. The passage continues in verses seven through 22 with numerous future tense phrases:

> He *is coming* out to lay your land waste. Your cities *will become* ruins and lie uninhabited. (*Jer 4:7*)

> "*When this happens*," says the LORD, "the king and his officials will lose their courage." (*Jer 4:9*)

> For messengers *are coming*, heralding disaster, from the city of Dan and from the hills of Ephraim. They are saying, 'Announce to the surrounding nations, "The enemy *is coming*!" Proclaim this message to Jerusalem: "Those who besiege cities *are coming* from a distant land. They are ready to raise the battle cry against the towns in Judah.' They *will surround* Jerusalem like men guarding a field because they have rebelled against me," says the LORD. (*Jer 4:15-17*)

> The LORD answered, "This *will happen* because my people are foolish. They do not know me." (*Jer 4:22*)

All of these passages indicate that a judgment was coming from the Lord in the future on parts of the nation of Israel. There is nothing in the passage that indicates the judgment took place in the ancient past. Then the passage in question:

> "I looked at the land and saw that it was an empty wasteland. I looked up at the sky, and its light had vanished. I looked at the mountains and saw that they were shaking. All the hills were swaying back and forth! I looked and saw that there were no more people, and that all the birds in the sky had flown away. I looked and saw that the fruitful land had become a desert and that all of the cities had been

> laid in ruins. The LORD had brought this all about because of his blazing anger. (*Jer 4:23-26*)

Jeremiah was shown in the spirit the destruction that the Lord was proclaiming on Judah and Jerusalem that was described in the preceding verses. In poetic fashion, the prophet compared Jerusalem and Judah to a barren wasteland with no sky, light, animals or people due to the devastating judgment that was coming. The very next verse confirms that the preceding four verses were to take place at a future time:

> *All this will happen* because the LORD said, "The whole land will be desolate; however, I will not completely destroy it." (*Jer 4:27*)

The most damaging aspect of The Gap Theory is that is requires four separate creations of Earth, where the scriptures only support three. Peter revealed in his second epistle that there will be three separate "worlds" occupying Earth, two of which are destroyed:

> For they deliberately suppress this fact, that by the word of God heavens existed long ago and an earth was formed out of water and by means of water. Through these things the world existing at that time [*world #1*] was destroyed when it was deluged with water. But by the same word the present heavens and earth [*world #2*] have been reserved for fire, by being kept for the day of judgment and destruction of the ungodly. (*II Pet 3:5-7*)

> But, according to his promise, we are waiting for new heavens and a new earth [*world #3*], in which righteousness truly resides. (*II Pet 3:13*)

Peter revealed the first world was created long ago and destroyed by the flood, and the second world is the one in which we currently live, which will be destroyed by fire. The third world will be created in the future, promised for believers.

But under the belief that there was a pre-Adamic world that was destroyed, *four* worlds would be required, not the three Peter identified in his inspired epistle. Because of this, I reject The Gap Theory as a mechanism for fitting an ancient fall of Lucifer into the Genesis chapter one creation narrative.

The Roles of Satan

In the scriptures that chronicle the involvement of Satan in God's plan for humanity, Satan is revealed to have three main roles: a tester or tempter, an adversary or hinderer, and a deceiver. These roles are interchangeable and complementary of each other.

Satan's role as a hinderer includes the ability to oppress both the physical and spiritual aspects of the human body. Physically, Satan can inflict pain, illness, and even death. Recall that Jesus revealed the source of the sickness of a woman whom he healed of a disability:

> And a woman was there who had been disabled by a spirit for eighteen years. She was bent over and could not straighten herself up completely. When Jesus saw her, he called her to him and said, "Woman, you are freed from your infirmity."
>
> "Then shouldn't this woman, a daughter of Abraham whom Satan bound for eighteen long years, be released from this imprisonment on the Sabbath day?" (*Luk 13:11-12; 16*)

Though Satan is able to attack the physical body, Jesus stated that we should not fear the one who could destroy the physical body. This is a reference to Satan's ability to kill, displayed when he killed the children of Job, for example. From a spiritual or mental perspective, Satan attacks the mind, will, and intellect with addiction and depression. The believer overcomes this attack by prayer and standing on the promises of God in his Word to deliver from evil.

Satan's multifaceted role as the one who would put God's people to the test through accusation and deception is clearly established from the beginning of Genesis. He put Eve to the test by deceiving her with a half-truth: that they would not die if they ate of the fruit of the Tree of the Knowledge of Good and Evil. Though they did not immediately die, they lost their immortal characteristics because they disobeyed God.

It is well known that Eve failed Satan's initial test, as did Adam, resulting in the introduction of disobedience and death to humanity. But there are many additional examples of throughout scripture Satan fulfilling his role as a tempter or tester of the loyalty of humanity to God. Take a minute to think of as many of them as you can, and then consider the following examples:

- The stalking and desired domination of Cain:

> Then the LORD said to Cain, "Why are you angry, and why is your expression downcast? Is it not true that if you do what is right, you will be fine? But if you do not do what is right, sin is crouching at the door. It desires to dominate you, but you must subdue it." (*Gen 4:6-7*)

> Not like Cain who was of the evil one and brutally murdered his brother. And why did he murder him? Because his deeds were evil, but his brother's were righteous. (*I Joh 3:12*)

The Lord revealed to Cain that he was being stalked by sin – that it was "crouching at the door" or lying in wait for him. According to *The International Standard Bible Encyclopedia*, the Hebrew word translated as Satan originates from the verb *sạṭan*, which means "to lie in wait." Clearly, Satan was the embodiment of sin, lying in wait for Cain and in a sense crouching at the door. As Cain was the firstborn son of Eve, perhaps Satan believed he was the prophesied seed of the woman that would crush his head, and he was constantly lying in wait to destroy Cain's life. John revealed in his first epistle that Cain was "of the evil one" because he made a decision to commit sin. As we know, Cain failed the test and killed his brother Abel. With the testing of Cain, Satan had put to the test each of the first three human beings, and all three had failed.

- The testing of Job to curse God if all was taken from him:

> Then the LORD said to Satan, "Have you considered my servant Job? For there is no one like him on the earth, a pure and upright man, one who fears God and turns away from evil. And he still holds firmly to his integrity, so that you stirred me up to destroy him without reason." But Satan answered the LORD, "Skin for skin! Indeed, a man will give up all that he has to save his life! But extend your hand and strike his bone and his flesh, and he will no doubt curse you to your face!" So the LORD said to Satan, "All right, he is in your power; only preserve his life." So Satan went out from the presence of the LORD, and he afflicted Job with a malignant ulcer from the sole of his feet to the top of his head. (*Job 2:3-7*)

Notice that God introduced the idea that Job was to be "considered" by Satan. Considered for what? For testing, by his agent of testing – Satan. Only then did Satan accuse Job of unfaithfulness and request to put him to the test. In this case, God used Satan to test his faithful servant, Job. Although Satan had evil intentions for the test, God had good intentions. Job proved to remain faithful, and God restored him to a place far better than his original state.

- The testing of King David to take an inventory of the size of his army:

> An adversary [Hb. *śậṭân*] opposed Israel, inciting David to count how many warriors Israel had. (*I Chr 21:1*)

The lack of a definite article in the Hebrew text caused the translators of the NET Bible to render the opening of the verse with "an adversary" where other translations render the opening with "Satan." In either case, it is likely, considering the parallel passage from I Kings, that God wanted David to be put to the test. Similar to the testing of Job, God may have used Satan himself or an agent of Satan to accomplish the test. David's failure of this test brought a severe plague upon the land of Israel that caused 70,000 people to die.

- The accusation against Joshua the high priest:

> Next I saw Joshua the high priest standing before the angel of the LORD, with Satan standing at his right hand to accuse him. The LORD said to Satan, "May the LORD rebuke you, Satan! May the LORD, who has chosen Jerusalem, rebuke you! Isn't this man like a burning stick snatched from the fire?" (*Zec 3:1-2*)

Similar to the accusation of Job, Satan attempted to accuse Joshua before the Lord. This time, however, the Lord did not allow it and instead issued a rebuke to Satan. This marks the final time Satan is mentioned in the Old Testament, and each time he is mentioned, it is in the role of testing and deception.

- The temptation of Jesus Christ at the beginning of his ministry:

> Then Jesus, full of the Holy Spirit, returned from the Jordan River and was led by the Spirit in the wilderness, where for forty days he endured temptations from the devil. He ate nothing during those days, and when they were completed, he was famished. (*Luk 4:1-2*)

This is the first mention of Satan in the New Testament, and it marked the ultimate test of humanity: the testing of Jesus Christ in the wilderness. In each of the three recorded temptations, Jesus conquered Satan's scheme by quoting Old Testament scriptures.

- The demand of Satan to sift the 11 disciples, just prior to the prediction that Simon Peter would three times deny that he knew Jesus:

> "Simon, Simon, pay attention! Satan has demanded to have you all, to sift you like wheat, but I have prayed for you, Simon, that your faith may not fail. When you have turned back, strengthen your brothers." (*Luk 22:31-32*)

- The fall of Ananias and Sapphira, who were deceived by Satan to lie to the Holy Spirit regarding whether they had given all of the proceeds from the sale of their land to the apostles:

> But Peter said, "Ananias, why has Satan filled your heart to lie to the Holy Spirit and keep back for

> yourself part of the proceeds from the sale of the land?" (*Act 5:3*)

- The testing of Satan in the life of believers:

> Do not deprive each other, except by mutual agreement for a specified time, so that you may devote yourselves to prayer. Then resume your relationship, so that Satan may not tempt you because of your lack of self-control. (*I Cor 7:5*)

> So when I could bear it no longer, I sent to find out about your faith, for fear that the tempter somehow tempted you and our toil had proven useless. (*I The 3:5*)

> Do not be afraid of the things you are about to suffer. The devil is about to have some of you thrown into prison so you may be tested, and you will experience suffering for ten days. Remain faithful even to the point of death, and I will give you the crown that is life itself. (*Rev 2:10*)

- The testing and hindering of the apostle Paul:

> For we wanted to come to you (I, Paul, in fact tried again and again) but Satan thwarted us. (*I The 2:18*)

> For even if I wish to boast, I will not be a fool, for I would be telling the truth, but I refrain from this so that no one may regard me beyond what he sees in me or what he hears from me, even because of the extraordinary character of the revelations. Therefore, so that I would not become arrogant, a thorn in the flesh was given to me, a messenger of Satan to

> trouble me — so that I would not become arrogant. (*I Cor 12:6-7*)

These many examples prove, over and over again, that Satan fulfilled the role of a tempter, an adversary, and a deceiver of God's people, to test their loyalty. In a few instances, the one being tested was victorious, but most of the time, the tests were failed. How does Satan accomplish these tests? Why is he so effective in his tests, not only against unbelievers, but against God's chosen people?

The New Testament reveals the depth of Satan's hatred of humanity. After his defeat by Jesus Christ at the cross, Satan turned his attention toward Christ's followers. He has no shortage of deceptive devices which highlight his ability to attack the spiritual and mental makeup of humanity:

- ...the evil one comes and snatches what was sown in his heart... (*Mat 13:19*)
- ...the spirit that is now energizing the sons of disobedience... (*Eph 2:2*)
- ...stand against the schemes of the devil. (*Eph 6:11*)
- ...the flaming arrows of the evil one. (*Eph 6:16*)
- ...so that we may not be exploited by Satan (for we are not ignorant of his schemes). (*II Cor 2:11*)
- ...the god of this age has blinded the minds of those who do not believe... (*II Cor 4:4*)
- ...even Satan disguises himself as an angel of light. (*II Cor 11:14*)
- ...escape the devil's trap where they are held captive to do his will. (*II Tim 2:26*)
- ...set free those who were held in slavery all their lives by their fear of death. (*Heb 2:15*)
- Your enemy the devil, like a roaring lion, is on the prowl looking for someone to devour. (*I Pet 5:8*)

Praise God that believers are not be ignorant of the devil's schemes. Through the dynamic power of the Holy Spirit living in us, Satan and his kingdom must flee. The believer is on the offensive, taking ground in the devil's territory through prayer and evangelism. We are more than conquerors through Jesus Christ and the proclamation of his cross!

Satan's Future Agenda

Having examined Satan's role in the world as an instrument of God to test the loyalty of his people through deceptive schemes, we now have a general understanding of his progression through history. In the beginning, Satan was both on the earth and in the heavenly realm, able to access the throne room of God. When asked by the Lord where he was before the testing of Job, Satan answered that he was walking about in the earth.

But as we examined in a previous chapter, there came a point in time when Satan was expelled from the heavenly throne room forever. There was a battle in the heavenly realm, and Satan and his kingdom were hurled to the earth as Jesus Christ ascended to the right hand of God to be the believer's advocate, interceding on our behalf before the Father. This expulsion from the heavenly realm took place during the time Jesus Christ was on the earth:

> Now is the judgment of this world; now the ruler of this world will be driven out. (*Joh 12:31*)

> Then I heard a loud voice in heaven saying, "The salvation and the power and the kingdom of our God, and the ruling authority of his Christ, have now come, because the accuser of our brothers and sisters, the one who accuses them day and night before our God, has been thrown down. (*Rev 12:10*)

From this time forward, there was a documented change in Satan's demeanor. Having realized he had been thoroughly defeated, he became filled with a great anger:

> "Therefore you heavens rejoice, and all who reside in them! But woe to the earth and the sea because the devil has come down to you! He is filled with terrible anger, for he knows that he only has a little time!" (*Rev 12:12*)

Satan was filled with terrible anger because he was henceforth denied access to the throne room of God. He was defrocked of his role as the accuser in the heavenly realm. But there was even more reason for him to be filled with hatred, because it was at this point that Satan realized he had been used by God in bringing to pass his secret plan, hidden from the foundation of the world:

> Disarming the rulers and authorities, he has made a public disgrace of them, triumphing over them by the cross. (*Col 2:15*)

The apostle Paul explained that it was in the cross of Jesus Christ that Satan's kingdom of evil was brought to ridicule. Satan did not know the secret of the sinless blood shed on the cross of Jesus Christ. It was by this blood that Jesus Christ entered the Most Holy Place of heaven and forever cleansed it, meaning that Satan no longer had any place to stand. His accusations became useless and void before Jesus Christ, our high priest:

> So it was necessary for the sketches of the things in heaven to be purified with these sacrifices, but the heavenly things themselves required better sacrifices than these. For Christ did not enter a sanctuary made with hands — the representation of the true

> sanctuary — but into heaven itself, and he appears now in God's presence for us. (*Heb 9:23-24*)

Confined to the earth and full of terrible anger because of the knowledge that God subjected him to a public disgrace, Satan began a ferocious campaign of deception which has continued now for almost 2,000 years.

The Ultimate, Final Deception

Satan's last stand and most brutal display of deception, however, is still to come. In one of the most important passages of prophecy in the New Testament, the apostle Paul revealed in his second epistle to the Thessalonians that Satan will energize a man of lawlessness:

> The arrival of the lawless one will be by Satan's working [Gr. *enérgeia*] with all kinds of miracles and signs and false wonders, and with every kind of evil deception directed against those who are perishing, because they found no place in their hearts for the truth so as to be saved. (*II The 2:9-10*)

Basically, Satan will pull out all the stops with the arrival of the lawless one. Satan will energize this man with four powerful devices: false miracles, signs, wonders, and every kind of evil deception. Notice that these devices are leveled at those who are perishing, unbelievers who found no place in their heart to believe the truth of the gospel.

It is likely that the stage for Satan's final deception began to be set in the twentieth century with the intense proliferation of aliens and unidentified flying objects (UFO's) in the media, especially movies and television. My belief is that these demonic phenomena will be part of the final grand deception, perhaps in concert with human intervention. More recently, the rise in popularity of vampirism, ghosts, mediums, witchcraft, and other forms of forbidden supernatural phenomena will serve to prepare a generation saturated in every form of evil for the ultimate Satanic deception to come.

Believers will not be affected by this deception. The next verse reveals that it will be in God's will to allow this to happen to unbelievers:

> Consequently God sends on them a deluding influence so that they will believe what is false. And so all of them who have not believed the truth but have delighted in evil will be condemned. (*I The 2:11-12*)

This is one of the saddest passages of scripture, because it reveals that in the future, God will purposely use Satan's deceptive devices to send a powerful delusion over unbelievers, so that they will put their trust in false miracles, signs, and wonders. Their fate will be sealed, and there will not be an opportunity for them to be saved.

Satan's final destination is revealed in The Revelation of Jesus Christ. In the future, there will be a period of time after which Satan is no longer able to deceive the nations of the earth. John the Revelator saw in a vision the binding of Satan and his expulsion to the abyss:

> He seized the dragon — the ancient serpent, who is the devil and Satan — and tied him up for a thousand years. The angel then threw him into the abyss and locked and sealed it so that he could not deceive the nations until the one thousand years were finished. (After these things he must be released for a brief period of time.) (*Rev 20:2-3*)

Near the end of this period of time, Satan will be released from the abyss. He will once again be able to deceive the nations in preparation for the final battle:

> Now when the thousand years are finished, Satan will be released from his prison and will go out to deceive the nations at the four corners of the earth, Gog and Magog, to bring them together for the battle. They are as numerous as the grains of sand in the sea. (*Rev 20:7-8*)

Satan's final defeat will take place at this battle. Although used by the Lord God throughout the ages, he will experience a brutal ending:

> And the devil who deceived them was thrown into the lake of fire and sulfur, where the beast and the false prophet are too, and they will be tormented there day and night forever and ever. (*Rev 20:10*)

Sadly, the lake of fire will have more occupants than these three entities. The same chapter reveals the fate of all those who do not have eternal life offered by faith in Jesus Christ:

> If anyone's name was not found written in the book of life, that person was thrown into the lake of fire. (*Rev 20:15*)

For those who suppose that they, or their family and friends, will be able to make a decision to follow Jesus Christ in the future (perhaps after the future catching-up and resurrection of the dead in Christ), the passage from II Thessalonians chapter two makes it clear that will not be an option. The time is now to believe the gospel and be saved. The time is now to have a change of mind toward God, to submit to his son Jesus Christ as the King of Kings, and trust in his sacrifice for sins.

The final chapter will explore the philosophical questions that arise if the origin of Satan as presented in this book is correct. If God created the devil for the purpose of testing the loyalty of his people, does this make God the author of evil in the world? Why would God even need to create a being like this? These questions and many more will be addressed in the final chapter.

11

THE PROBLEM OF EVIL

It is widely agreed by Christian scholars and teachers that the most difficult questions for a Christian to answer involve the problem of evil. Many treatises have been written throughout the ages by individuals much more gifted than myself, attempting to provide answers to the difficult questions about how a good God could allow evil to exist in the world. The answers are not easy, and as a result, an effort is made to in some way shift the blame away from God. I believe this is the primary motivating factor in the development of the myth of Lucifer.

An Attempt to Defend God

Think about it: when an unbeliever asks why a good, all-knowing God allows evil and suffering in the world, what is the answer? Consider the following hypothetical conversation between a Christian and an atheist:

> "If God really exists, how could a *good* God allow evil and suffering in the world?" asks the atheist.
>
> The Christian answers, "Well, God created everything good in the beginning. But an angel named Lucifer became proud and rebelled sometime in the ancient past, became Satan, and introduced evil into God's perfect, sinless creation."

Answering in this way, the Christian believes that he has successfully defended God from being the source of evil. Lucifer becomes responsible for all the evil in the world and God is absolved of guilt.

Why does the Christian respond in this way? Because he is taught from an early age that Satan was once a fallen angel named Lucifer who became filled with pride and was cast out of heaven. He feels he must defend God from being responsible for evil, because, well, God is a good God and did not want evil to be present in the world from the beginning.

But even if the myth of Lucifer's rebellion were true, it still would not accomplish the desired absolution of God for the origin of evil in the world. Continuing the earlier conversation between the atheist and the Christian:

> "Umm, Lucifer…okay, but couldn't God have avoided Lucifer's rebellion by just not creating him in the first place? No Lucifer, no evil in the world, right?" reasons the atheist. "Or, even if he created Lucifer and allowed him to fall, couldn't he have just destroyed him *before* he was able to deceive Adam and Eve?"
>
> The Christian thoughtfully pauses. *How do I answer this? Hmm…wait! What if God didn't know*

> *that Lucifer would fall? That would put the blame back on Lucifer!* But just before blurting it out, the Christian remembers that God is all-knowing, declaring the end from the beginning. Thus, the Christian realizes there is no satisfactory answer to the atheist's challenge.
>
> Noticing the pregnant pause and the Christian's struggle to come up with an answer, the atheist continues, "It seems to me that, any way you slice it, God *is* responsible for evil in the world, or at least for allowing it to exist."

The atheist is correct. Why? Because the fact remains that Satan still exists in the world, and God allows him to exist, whether he was created good and fell, or whether he was evil from the beginning. Even if God made a good angel named Lucifer knowing that he would fall, he could have vaporized him from existence to avoid the introduction of evil. But the all-powerful, all-knowing God allowed him to exist and bring about the fall of humanity.

One explanation I've heard to reply to the atheist's challenge is that Satan is a spirit being, and because all spirit beings are eternal by nature, God could not vaporize Satan out of existence. To do so would contradict his established spiritual laws. But Revelation chapter 20 reveals that an angel will be responsible for casting Satan into the abyss so that he can no longer deceive the nations. If an angel can do this, then certainly an all-powerful God could render Satan inoperable or completely vaporize him if he wanted to do so.

Allowing Evil to Exist

You see, whether God (a) made Satan originally good, or (b) made him predisposed to evil, he is still responsible for Satan's existence in the universe. Because God allows Satan to exist, he apparently has a use for him in his ultimate plan. This was examined thoroughly in the previous chapter, as the scriptures reveal that God allows Satan to exist as a tester of the loyalty of his people. It is a fact of scripture that we must live with: *God has a use for Satan*. If God has no use for him and did not want him to be around to ruin his perfect creation, he would never have allowed him to exist, either as a fallen angel or as a spiritual entity predisposed to evil.

If God wanted to create a world with no evil, he could have created beings that would never have the option of disobeying his commands, such as animals. But by creating moral entities which have the option to obey or disobey, such as angels and humans, God is responsible for at least *allowing* evil to exist in the universe. He allowed a spirit to go to Ahab and lie to him. He allowed Satan to kill Job's family and afflict Job. He allowed an evil spirit to come against King Saul. He allowed Satan to test David to take a census of his army, resulting in the deaths of thousands of Israelites. He allowed an agent of Satan to come against Paul, so that Paul's weakness would result in the exaltation of God's power in his life. The key is that God *allowed* these things to achieve his sovereign purposes.

Consider what the author of Proverbs stated about the Lord's use for the wicked:

> The LORD works everything for its own ends — *even the wicked* for the day of disaster. (*Pro 16:4*)

Does the writer here attempt to defend God for allowing evil in the world? On the contrary, the Lord has a purpose for the wicked and evil that exists in the world, and he does not defend himself from the charge of being responsible for it. That includes Satan, who introduced evil actions into the world. Although God created Satan as a being predisposed to evil, God does not commit acts of evil himself. Satan is not co-equal with God. He is not God's alter ego or his evil twin. He is a created being predisposed to evil, engaging in acts of evil and deceiving the world to engage in the same acts.

Another passage in Deuteronomy reveals something about the character of God that may help to further explain why he created Satan and allows evil to exist in the world. When establishing the laws for his people, he delivered the following message to Moses:

> Suppose a prophet or one who foretells by dreams should appear among you and show you a sign or wonder, and the sign or wonder should come to pass concerning what he said to you, namely, "Let us follow other gods" — gods whom you have not previously known — "and let us serve them." You must not listen to the words of that prophet or dreamer, for the LORD your God *will be testing you* to see if you love him with all your mind and being. (*Deu 13:1-3*)

God told Moses that if false prophets were to rise among them using signs and wonders that were not from God, they must be ignored. But God did not say they should be ignored because they were demonic, or because Satan was inspiring them. Rather, it was because God was testing his people to see if they fully loved him.

Why does God do this? Is someone making him do this? No, it is because testing the loyalty of his people is *part of his character*. It is for that purpose that he sovereignly created Satan and allows him to exist.

Clearly, God could have created beings which had no option of being disloyal, but would robotically follow everything he commanded. But how precious and cherished would that loyalty be? It would be of no value whatsoever. It would be pointless to create humanity with the capability of being disobedient, but with no medium to provide the option of disobedience. God sovereignly chose to create Satan as the medium that would introduce the option of disobedience.

God already had animals which act upon their instincts, such as bees creating hives, beavers building dams, ants gathering food, and birds flying south during the winter. He did not desire another predictable, mechanical creation, but rather a moral creation that would choose to love and obey him above other options. If there is no option but to obey, the obedience is meaningless, robotic, emotionless, and of no value.

We are called to be loyal to God in the midst of a world seduced by Satan. We must bring people out of the darkness of this world and share the news of Jesus Christ's conquest over Satan's kingdom through his sinless blood. God ordained this paradigm, a type of contest for his sentient, moral creation, and servants of the King proclaim his sovereignty, love, and power through the power of the Holy Spirit. God sovereignly chose to install Satan as the one who would battle the Lord Jesus Christ and his servants, but he will ultimately lose the battle.

This does not make God the author of evil in the world. Certainly Satan is an evil being, which is made clear in the scriptures. But the evil acts do not originate with God and are certainly not committed by him. They are committed by moral beings which choose to listen to the inducement of Satan and then commit the acts of evil. This began with Eve in the Garden of Eden when Satan offered an option that was contrary to God's command. Is God responsible for that? He is responsible for the presence of Satan *to offer the option* of disobedience, but he is not responsible for Adam and Eve's choice of that option.

The Problem of Evil – Solved

So, let us revisit the conversation between the atheist and the Christian. Given the preceding discussion, how would the conversation progress differently than before?

"If God really exists, how could a *good* God allow evil and suffering in the world?" asks the atheist.

"God allows suffering because his special, moral creation chose to disobey his command. The result of that disobedience introduced evil actions into his perfect, sinless world," the Christian replies.

The atheist thoughtfully considers this unexpected response, considering how to reply. "Okay, but 'the devil made them do it,' right? I mean, couldn't God have just wiped out the devil and avoided all the pain and suffering he caused?"

The Christian says, "Oh, so you believe in the devil, but not God?"

"Uh, well, no…I was just anticipating your response…"

"But you said it yourself – you blamed the devil for the evil in the world." The Christian notices the atheist is a bit perturbed by this, but continues.

"God created Satan for his sovereign purpose, to test the loyalty of his people, and they failed the test."

"See!" the atheist blurts out with eyes wide. "It's God's fault for creating Satan. If he wouldn't have created Satan, none of this would have happened."

"Wait a minute – are you an atheist or not? You are making an argument involving God, a being you don't even believe exists."

"But I was just anticipating…"

"You've done that twice now, and both times you've anticipated incorrectly," the Christian interrupts with a wry smile. "Satan exists in God's sovereign plan to provide the option of disobedience.

We are not robots…we are a moral, sentient creation with the ability to choose, and Satan's existence makes our choices *meaningful and valuable* to God."

"Come again? Satan's existence makes our choices valuable to God?" the atheist asks, now visibly confused.

"That's right. If God would have designed his special creation without the ability to choose, our obedience would have been meaningless – robotic. Satan's role was to *offer the choice*, and when we shun his evil schemes, that choice is meaningful in God's sight and brings him glory."

The atheist feels he is losing control of the conversation, because it is not going where he expected. "But Adam and Eve made the wrong choice!"

"That's right, and that is the reason there is evil in the world. God allows both evil and good, because he designed us to make choices, and he designed Satan as a choice provider. By the way, I'm surprised you believe in Adam and Eve, too."

"I've never had it explained to me like this before," says the atheist, staring off into space. He scarcely noticed the Adam and Eve taunt.

The Christian concludes, "You see, in God's sovereign plan, he became a man, sending Jesus Christ into the world to take the punishment for Adam and Eve's evil choice and make payment for it. But not just for their evil choice, but all of our evil choices. His death on the cross covers all the sin of the world, and his resurrection from the dead *proved* he is God. As for Satan, Jesus Christ came into the world to destroy his works, and he will be

> extinguished in the lake of fire when God no longer has a use for him in his sovereign plan."
>
> The atheist realizes that this Christian is different, and it is time to move on. But he does so with a new appreciation for God and his sovereign plan.

This conversation is much more fruitful than the first! Not only is the problem of evil answered in a satisfactory fashion, but the gospel message is able to be combined with the answer. The awkward position in which the Christian found himself in the first conversation in attempting to answer using the myth of Lucifer is avoided completely. The second conversation and outcome is very possible if we allow God's sovereignty to shine through instead of trying to shift the blame off of him and onto Lucifer.

Conclusion

Paul revealed in his letter to the Roman believers that it is in God's character to create a vessel meant for a special purpose, even one that would ultimately be the object of his wrath:

> Has the potter no right to make from the same lump of clay one vessel for special use and another for ordinary use? But what if God, willing to demonstrate his wrath and to make known his power, has endured with much patience *the objects of wrath* prepared for destruction? (*Rom 9:21-22*)

While this passage has nothing to do with Satan's origin, it does reveal why God allows the existence of evil in the world. A feature of God's sovereignty is his allowance of "objects of wrath" to exist and be ultimately destroyed. This was to demonstrate his wrath and showcase his power. The quintessential "object of wrath" is Satan, whose creation would not only serve to showcase God's wrath and power, but most importantly his love for humanity in sending Jesus Christ to destroy his works.

With excruciating detail, this book has chronicled the history of the tradition of Lucifer throughout the early centuries after Jesus' resurrection and ascension to heaven. At the heart of its development, by honest, well-intentioned men of God, was the desire to answer the question of the origin of evil in the world. It was even developed using the scriptures, but those scriptures do not teach what those men said they teach.

We should not allow the desire to insulate God from the responsibility of allowing evil to exist in the world to cause us to blame it on the myth of a rogue angel. God does not attempt to insulate himself from the charge of either allowing evil or using it for his sovereign agenda, as is evident in the passages above. As we saw with the conversation between the atheist and the Christian, this method does not answer the important philosophical questions we hope it will. In addition, it puts God in the awkward position of having to wait for one of his angels to rebel instead of simply from the beginning creating a being that would provide the option of disobedience to, and test the loyalty of, God's special creation made in his own image: humanity.

God's sovereign purpose in creating Satan and allowing him to exist to the present time is perfectly declared by John in his first epistle:

> The one who practices sin is of the devil, because the devil has been sinning from the beginning. For this purpose the Son of God was revealed: to destroy the works of the devil. (*I Joh 3:8*)

While the Bible does not provide all the details we desire regarding the origin of Satan, I believe this verse provides all the data the Holy Spirit requires us to know about it. John succinctly defines both the beginning and the end of Satan. From the beginning, he was a sinful creature, and in the end, he will be destroyed by the Lord Jesus Christ. This is a promise of scripture that I hold dear: the enemy of my soul will be destroyed by its Savior, the Lord Jesus Christ!

Then His Voice Shook the Earth...

Mount Sinai, the Trumpet of God, and the Resurrection of the Dead in Christ

ISBN: 978-0-6151-3614-1

Then his voice shook the earth, but now he has promised, "I will once more shake not only the earth but heaven too." (*Heb 12:26*)

Does this verse contain a key to understanding the mystery of the last trumpet that will sound at the resurrection of the dead in Christ? Serving pastors, scholars, and the laity, *Then His Voice Shook the Earth* presents provocative new exegesis of the resurrection to immortality, the trumpet of God, and the power that will accompany this colossal future event. In addition, an important connection between the first century ascension of Jesus Christ to the right hand and Revelation chapter four through six will bring new meaning to the opening of the seven-sealed scroll.

"*This book reveals an important breakthrough concerning the meaning of the last trumpet. Lowe's work is a breath of fresh air among the established field of eschatology.*"

– Peter D. Goodgame, author of *Red Moon Rising- The Rapture and the Timeline of the Apocalypse*

Made in the USA
Monee, IL
07 September 2020

41134468R00115